Larkin at Work

LARKIN AT WORK

A Study of Larkin's Mode of Composition as seen in his Workbooks

by
A.T. Tolley

THE
UNIVERSITY
OF HULL
PRESS

Acknowledgements

The workbooks, manuscripts and quotes are and remain copyright of the Estate of Philip Larkin and are reproduced with the permission of the Trustees.

The photograph of Philip Larkin is the copyright of the University of Hull Photographic Services Unit.

First published by

The University of Hull Press
Cottingham Road
Hull
HU6 7RX

and

The Philip Larkin Society

© A. T. Tolley 1997

British Library cataloguing in publication data
A catalogue record for this book is available from the British Library

ISBN 0 85958 661 8 *hardback*
ISBN 0 85958 662 6 *paperback*

Printed in Great Britain by
Advanced Laser Press, Longstanton, Cambridge

Other books by A.T. Tolley

The Early Published Poems of Stephen Spender: A Chronology
The Poetry of the Thirties
The Poetry of the Forties
My Proper Ground: A Study of the Work of Philip Larkin
and Its Development

Edited by A.T. Tolley

John Lehmann: A Tribute
Roy Fuller: A Tribute
The Literary Essays of John Heath-Stubbs

For

STEPHANIE

CONTENTS

ACKNOWLEDGEMENTS

My first debt is to the late Philip Larkin who read some of the material incorporated in this book, gave permission for its publication and provided information. I am also deeply indebted to his literary executors, Andrew Motion and Anthony Thwaite, not only for permission to publish the copyright material from the Larkin Workbooks and material from their own work on Larkin, but for conversation and correspondence that have been valuable in preparing the book. The workbooks and letters of Philip Larkin are and remain the copyright of the Estate of Philip Larkin and are reproduced here with the Trustees' kind permission. Anthony Thwaite's edition of Larkin's *Collected Poems* and of his *Selected Letters* and Andrew Motion's *Philip Larkin: A Writer's Life* have been valuable and constant sources of reference; as has B.J. Bloomfield's *Philip Larkin: A Bibliography*. Others who have been helpful are Maeve Brennan, James Booth and John White. Further debts will, I hope, be clear from material acknowledged in the text; though I should mention that the studies of the Yeats manuscripts by Jon Stallworthy and Curtis Bradford have provided important models for me in the presentation of my work.

I have received most generous assistance throughout my work from Brian Dyson and the staff of the University Archives in the Brynmor Jones Library at the University of Hull. I have also benefitted from the services of the staff of the Manuscript Room at the British Library.

The Social Science and Humanities Research Council of Canada gave me a Release Time Grant that greatly expedited my work. Michael Gnarowski of Carleton University Press, as ever, gave valuable encouragement. I am grateful to James Booth and the Larkin Society for their interest and support in this project.

Christina Thiele of the Carleton Production Centre prepared the camera-ready copy of the difficult text. My wife, Glenda, made many helpful suggestions.

Some of the material in this book first appeared in *Arc* and was used in a different form in my earlier study, *My Proper Ground*. Some of the thoughts in that book inevitably emerge in this one. I am grateful to the publishers for acceptance of any such reappearance. The texts of poems by Philip Larkin appear by permission of his publishers, Faber and the Marvell Press.

PREFATORY NOTE

The texts reproduced in this book are based on transcriptions from Philip Larkin's workbooks in the British Library and the Larkin Archive at the University of Hull. While these workbooks were used in a very orderly manner, the writing was done in pencil; and Larkin frequently crossed out work very vigorously. Some of what he wrote can never be regained; and it must be remembered that a certain amount of what is transcribed here represents only the careful conjecture of one reader.

These caveats should be kept in mind in any examination of the pattern of the transcriptions. Attempt has been made to reproduce as closely as possible the physical relationship of the words in the manuscripts. However, that relationship is often very difficult to discern in heavily worked over passages, where corrections have been inserted wherever space permitted. The reproduction of the transcribed texts employs a format that attempts to give order to the relationship of the various words in any passage. For instance, words that stand above other words in the manuscript are placed in the line above; though, in the workbooks, they may be sneaked in between lines. The disposition of material is thus clearer and more systematic than it appears to be in the workbooks; though it is hoped that the relationship is hence more comprehensible. Crossing out of words is reproduced by putting a line through the words concerned; and the continuity of crossings-out in the workbooks is respected. Extended passages that were crossed out in any way in the workbooks have a diagonal line through them. Passages crossed out by Larkin in a way that makes them undecipherable are represented by a question mark with a horizontal line through it (-?-). Question marks in Larkin's text that are independently crossed out are represented by a question mark with a diagonal line through it (⁊).

Chapter 1

THE WORKBOOKS

"So wie dem Meister manchmal das eilig/nähere Blatt den *wirk-lichen* Strich/abnimmt . . . " ("As sometimes the hurriedly nearer leaf/catches the *authentic stroke* from the master's/hand . . . "): so wrote Rilke in *Sonnette an Orpheus* (Zweiter Teil, 2).[1] The handiest paper often caught the inspiration of poets; and sometimes those pieces of paper survived to give us a record of the composition of a poem, as was the case with Yeats's drafts. More frequently a poet's earliest sketches got discarded, sometimes in favour of completed versions of the poem, typescripts of which are quite often what one finds in manuscript collections in libraries. Very few poets have left a complete and systematically maintained collection of all the draftings of their poetry. Even the celebrated notebooks of Dylan Thomas are "good copy" books, containing what Thomas took to be final versions of his early poems. Philip Larkin's workbooks contain his work on almost every known poem by him written after the time that he began using those workbooks. They thus constitute a rare record of the complete drafting of the poems of a major poet over his entire mature life. It would seem that it was Larkin's intention that this should be the case. He belonged to the Arts Council's Poetry Manuscript Committee and campaigned vigorously to have modern British literary manuscripts stay in their country of origin.[2] The purpose of this book is to explore what the workbooks show of the process of composition as carried out by Larkin; and, as a corollary, to further the general understanding of how poetry is composed.

Larkin probably began using the books around December 1943; though the sequence of entries begins in October 1944. The last entry is probably from November 1980. There are eight workbooks in all, each containing about one hundred leaves. Aside from photographs and quotations in the covers, the books contain almost nothing except draft poems by Larkin; though quite a substantial number of sheets, mainly typescripts or printed versions of poems, are tipped in. The drafting is accompanied on some pages by drawings and doodles, which do not seem to be related to the poetry in most cases; and there is the occasional note by Larkin to himself. A complete bibliographical description of the workbooks is given in the section, "A Note on Sources".

The books were used in a methodical way from the beginning to the end. Poems are regularly dated, mainly only on completion; and discarded material is regularly crossed out. However, from around April 1959, Larkin appears to have begun dating pages; though his most common practice in the later workbooks seems to have been to start a new page when he came back to a poem on a new day and to date that page. The entries were evidently written with what Larkin once facetiously called "a succession of Royal Sovereign 2B pencils".[3] The poems appear chronologically in the order in which they were undertaken, and there is very little interlocking of drafts of different poems, and few blank spaces.

All this would seem to substantiate the sense that what we have is Larkin's complete work on every poem in the workbooks, and that no manuscript drafting was done outside the books. Almost no sheets containing manuscript drafting of Larkin's poems are known to exist. The one limitation to this conclusion is explained in Larkin's own words: "when the poem is finished I type it out, and sometimes make small alterations."[4] In the case of some poems, particularly in the earlier workbooks, Larkin made fair copies in the workbook. However, in most cases he seems to have drafted his poems to a point where the corrected manuscript represented his final intentions. A careful scrutiny of the final corrected versions of such poems in the workbooks reveals that, despite the complexity of correction in some instances, they represent the text almost as printed. However, in other cases, Larkin appears to have made further corrections when he took the poem to the typewriter; and of this work we have little or no record, though some typescripts exist.

There have been many literary appreciations of Larkin's poetry; and while the workbook drafts may seem in some cases to throw light on how the poems are to be received, this book will not aim to offer readings of *Collected Poems* in the light of what we find in the workbooks — or only in so far as such comment assists the study of the process of composition, which is the purpose of this book. The overall stylistic development of Larkin's poetry was the subject of my earlier book, *My Proper Ground*; and this too will be the subject of comment only in so far as it illuminates the process of composition.

It is, of course, not possible in a single book to discuss the drafting of all of Larkin's published poems. Certain major poems have been selected, along with shorter ones representative of the various periods of his work and representative of various aspects of the composition of his poems. As the poems appear in the workbooks more or less in chronological order, their sequence is not described, as this is shown in Anthony Thwaite's edition of *Collected Poems*. The workbooks contain a large number of uncompleted poems; and there are a small number of poems that seem to have been regarded by Larkin, at some point, as being completed, but which do not appear in *Collected Poems*. These, too, will not be described here. The material, in both cases, is of such extent that it could be the subject of separate study.

The drafting of some poems is given in its entirety; but, in the case of some of the major poems, the length of the drafting prohibits this. A complete reproduction of the drafting of these poems, without interpolated commentary, would merely leave the reader with the confusing task of sorting out how the drafting progresses — a task undertaken by this book. Some of the drafting of these poems shows Larkin circling around comparatively minor difficulties. Indeed, as will be seen, there are few major changes of direction as he composes; and major completed or near completed portions of poems are almost never set aside.

Finally, it should be remarked that not every aspect of the development of Larkin's mode of composition is revealed in full in the workbooks. His thinking is revealed only in what he wrote down or corrected. Unrecorded meditations will remain forever unrecorded. Nonetheless, it is hoped that what is given will provide not only an idea of the mode of composition, but also a full enough documentary account of what is to be seen in the workbooks, and that a sense of their richness and complexity will be conveyed.

Chapter 2

THE EARLY POEMS

Larkin probably began using the first Workbook in 1943, while he was still at St. John's College, Oxford — about a year before the compilation of *The North Ship*, published in 1945; the last entry is from March 1950, a year before the publication of *XX Poems* (1951). For most of this period, Larkin was librarian in Wellington in Shropshire, and the early portion of the Workbook corresponds to what he later described as "three years trying to write like Yeats".[1]

The first poem in this Workbook is "If grief could burn out", included in *The North Ship* as poem XVIII.

> If grief could burn out
> Like a sunken coal,
> The heart would rest quiet,
> The unrent soul
> Be still as a veil;
> But I have watched all night
>
> The fire grow silent,
> The grey ash soft:
> And I stir the stubborn flint
> The flames have left,
> And grief stirs, and the deft
> Heart lies impotent.

There are just two versions:

> If grief could burn out
> Like a sunken coal
> The heart would ~~be~~ rest
> ~~And leave the heart~~ quiet
> The unrent soul
> Be Still as a veil.
> But I have sat all night
>
> Watching the fire grow silent,
>   ash become
> The grey ~~ashes~~ / soft:
> And I stir the bits of flint
> That the flames have left,

The entire drafting is given of all the poems discussed in this chapter.

And grief stirs, and the deft
Heart lies impotent.

October 5th, 1944

If grief could burn out
Like a sunken coal,
The heart would rest quiet,
The unrent soul
Be still as a veil.
                watched
But I have ~~sat~~ all night

~~Watching~~ The fire grow silent,
The grey ash ~~become~~ soft:
And I stir the bits of flint
That the flames have left,
And grief stirs, and the deft
Heart lies impotent.

5.10.44

The changes from draft to draft are slight. The move from "And leave the heart quiet" to "The heart would rest quiet" gives a more arresting line and introduces the notion of "rest" — a change that evidently took place via the more commonplace phrase "would be quiet". These changes meant that "The unrent soul" was no longer the object of "leave", so that the verb "Be" had to be introduced into the fifth line. In the second stanza, "The grey ashes soft", may have seemed too light metrically, and the use of the understood verb "grow" a little awkward. Larkin changed the line to "The grey ash become soft"; but, after writing out his revised version, evidently perceived that replacing "sat . . . Watching" by "watched" would give a stronger final line to his first stanza and a firmer link into the second stanza, where the first two lines became the object of "watched". In addition, "The fire grow silent" is metrically smoother than "Watching the fire grow silent".

This discussion may seem to make heavy going of the relatively slight changes; and, if it does, it serves to highlight their slightness. The alterations result largely in an improvement of the movement of the poem — a feature of which Larkin, from his earliest compositions, showed undoubted mastery. The small amount of alteration — and the small number of drafts — was in fact characteristic of Larkin's mode of composition at this stage of his career; with the result that, as with so many of the poems in the first Workbook, little evidence is offered of the process of composition beyond the fact of Larkin's fluency. Larkin later spoke of his early habits of composition in a derisory way: "Every night after supper before opening my large green manuscript book I used to limber up by turning the pages of the 1933 plum-coloured Macmillan edition [of Yeats] . . . ";[2] and, while the results were better than this dismissive characterisation might suggest, Larkin included only two poems composed before 1948 when he brought together *The Less Deceived* in 1955 — "Going" and "Wedding-Wind". As will be seen, he evidently came to associate his early poems with an attitude towards poetry and its composition that he later rejected.

It is difficult to judge from a pencilled manuscript how much alteration has taken place by erasure; but it seems fair to say that there are quite a lot of earlier poems that did not undergo much alteration. In addition, to judge from the texts of uncompleted poems, there appears to have been little drafting ahead, with gaps in poems being filled in afterwards. Larkin does seem to have gone back over the Workbook at the end of 1946, possibly when he was preparing the typescript of his unpublished collection, *In the Grip of Light*, and there was some retrospective reworking. "Beggars" (with its Yeatsian refrain "The black cowl and the white cowl/Will not show us their faces") was dated "5-2-46" and then redated "6-10-46", evidently after revision; while "When the tide draws out" was dated "9/9/45" and "23/9/45", and later annotated by Larkin "corrected 6/10/46". Nonetheless, neither poem shows signs of major change; and neither was included in *In the Grip of Light*, though an annotated typescript of "When the tide draws out" is to be found in the Larkin archives.

Two early poems for which Larkin evidently had some regard at the time of composition were "Who whistled for the wind", completed 15th December 1945, and "That girl is lame", completed 13th November 1946. "Who whistled for the wind" was included in *In the Grip of Light*; and both are marked "Canto" in the notebook. This marking is there, not (as Larkin told Jenny Stratford) because "Canto" was an earlier title for *In the Grip of Light*,[3] but because (as Larkin later corrected himself) the poems in question had been sent to Arthur Ley, the prospective editor of *Canto*, a periodical that seems never to have appeared.[4]

> Who whistled for the wind, that it should break
> Gently, on this air?
> On what ground was it gathered, where
> For the carrying, for its own sake,
> Is night so gifted?

Mind never met
Image of death like this, and yet
(All winds crying for that unbroken field,
Day having lifted)
Black flowers burst out wherever the night has knelt.

Once again, these poems came with relative ease, as is illustrated
in the case of "Who whistled for the wind". Larkin seems to have
drafted the poem to his satisfaction on one page, dating it "14.12.45";
and then to have copied it out in a clean version the next day, with
one or two alterations to the last two lines, dating it "15.12.45".

Who whistled for the wind, that it should break
Gently on this air?
On
~~Off~~ what ground was it gathered, where
For the carrying, for its own sake,
Is ~~the~~ night ~~this~~ so gifted? ~~-?-~~ — faces and stays,
As if a hand had opened, and no mind
Ever met thoughts

Who whistled for the wind, that it should break
Gently on this air?
On what ground was it gathered, where
For the carrying, for its own sake,
Is night so gifted?
~~Image~~   ~~mind never met~~
~~Shaping Hinting~~   ~~and yet~~
~~Image of death like this, yet cannot alter mind~~
                    ~~cry~~   unbroken field
~~All winds are crying~~ now for that ~~-?- field~~
~~Of the black flowers~~
                    mind never met
Image of death like this, and yet
                          unbroken
(All winds ~~are~~ crying for that ~~untouched~~ field
Now day has lifted
~~Where morning never lifted~~
            new black flowers   night has knelt
Dreams of ~~black wildflowers~~ where the ~~wind / kneeled~~
                              14.12.45

Who whistled for the wind, that it should break,
Gently, on the air?
On what ground was it gathered, where
For the carrying, for its own sake,

Is night so giftcd?
                    Mind never met
Image of death like this, and yet
(All winds crying for that unbroken field,
Day having lifted)
                    burst out wherever the
Black flowers ~~creates, all where the~~ night has knelt.
                                        15.12.45

The opening lines came much as they stayed; while "no mind/Ever met thoughts" — the point at which Larkin first stopped — gets refocused in the second version as "mind never met/Image of death like this". As was to be characteristic of Larkin throughout his career, he attempts corrections of this new passage, only to retain much of his first shot when he writes the passage out again. The poem rhymes a/b/b/a/c/d/d/e/c/e; and all the rhymes are perfect, except in the last line, which one would think most important in this respect. Initially Larkin had "kneeled", rhyming with the earlier "field"; but a final correction changes this to the more natural "knelt".

The poem has the unfocused quality of some of the poems in *In the Grip of Light*; and one could be forgiven if one asked what conjunction of feelings the poem was attempting to bring into focus. The poem seems to operate as a collocation of certain verbal gestures that then had an emotive force for Larkin, as in the line, "All winds crying for that unbroken field", which seems little more than an occasion for bringing together the poetic associations of "all", "winds", "crying" and "unbroken". The corrections we encounter are, perhaps in consequence, relatively insubstantial: "All winds crying now for that" has "cry" substituted for "crying", only for the substitution to be rejected; while the "black flowers" in the last line undergo a number of transformations, presumably to fit the syntax. Yet Larkin thought well enough of the poem to submit it for publication — admittedly at a time when his poems, in contrast to his novels, were not getting printed.

"That girl is lame" is a better and slightly later poem.

~~Somewhere a bone is out of socket~~

That girl is lame: look at my rough
Hands. If there is skill enough
 On earth to   to
~~In the world to~~ ease the bone back ~~in~~ the socket,
Wishing is useless for I have not got it:
No human patience ever traced

misplaced
Wandering pain back to its ~~first~~
Home. And there to intercede
What flawless fingers I should need;
~~First I must be healed~~
Hands I have not; ~~all would then be thought~~
hands
~~And that requires so differen~~

That girl is lame: look at my rough
      Can there be
Hands. ~~Where is there~~ skill enough
On earth to ease the bone back to its place?
Is human patience wise enough to trace
Wandering pain? And were I allowed to find
         as sick a mind
Grief's mainspring could ~~a mind~~
        Among such roots to intercede
Give comfort? ~~What flawless fingers I should need~~
What flawless fingers I should need,
~~Among such tender roots to intercede~~;
Hands I have not, hands I could only gain
By such turning of the world from pain
That all would be renewed. And at that spring,
      look
She would not ~~turn~~ to me for anything.
              13.xi.1946

After drafting the first eight lines with little alteration, Larkin got into difficulty; and, in a manner characteristic of him all his life, wrote out again what he had already drafted, making alterations. These included the elimination of one line and the changing of others. With this second draft, the poem is complete, and the only changes in completing it are a rearrangement of phrases between two lines and the substitution of a word or phrase in three places. The possibility that his "rough hands" could have anything to do with curing the girl's lameness seems a bit of poetic posturing; and the poem is more a meditation on pain, grief and purity, and on Larkin's somewhat self-pitying sense that he lacks the high-toned purity that the poem conjures. Yet the movement of the poem is controlled and masterly; and Larkin again thought well enough of it to try to submit it for publication.

A typescript of the poem has survived, on which Larkin made manuscript changes, possibly at the time when publication seemed possible. "And" of the penultimate line becomes "But", while below the poem he wrote:

> so free from
> By an apprenticeship ~~untouched by~~ pain
> ~~have been~~
> ~~That all would be renewed, changed~~
> All wd have been ~~be as new~~
> ~~be~~ made new

It was evidently intended that the conclusion should read:

> By an apprenticeship so free from pain
> All would have been made new. But at that spring
> She would not look to me for anything.

The poem was not included in *Collected Poems*; and no final version exists. What we have shows Larkin arriving at a version that satisfied him after very little modification of his first phrasing.

Going

> There is an evening coming in
> Across the fields, one never seen before,
> That lights no lamps.
>
> Silken it seems at a distance, yet
> When it is drawn up over the knees and breast
> It brings no comfort.
>
> Where has the tree gone, that locked
> Earth to the sky? What is under my hands,
> That I cannot feel?
>
> What loads my hands down?

"Going", which Larkin kept in print all his life, is an example of an earlier poem that again seems to have come at once in very much its final shape, giving little evidence of its gestation. It appears in the corner of a page of the Workbook in the midst of the drafting of a poem, "Dig at the centre of the frost", that was never completed. Written early in 1946, it was published in *XX Poems* in 1951 and later in *The Less Deceived*. The following reproduces the complete working of the poem in the workbook:

> There
> ~~Here~~ is an evening coming in

                    one never seen before
Across the fields, ~~and in its path~~
That lights
~~It has   ?~~ — no lamps.

Silken it seems at distance; when
              up   breast
It is drawn / over the knees and ~~?~~
        brings no comfort
It ~~is harsh as sacking~~.

Where has the tree gone, that locks
Earth to the sky? What is under my hands
That I cannot feel ~~it~~?

What loads my hands down?

As will be seen, the corrected version is almost the published one.
The alterations do not change the overall impact of the poem, merely
strengthen it, as with "That lights no lamps" for the less sensuous
"It has no lamps". The replacement of "harsh as sacking" by "brings
no comfort" does not alter the basic tenor of the line, but prevents
the over-realization of the cloth image implicit in "drawn up over
the knees". "There" for "Here" enhances the feeling of distance and
elusiveness important to the poem. It is one of Larkin's relatively few
poems in free verse.

Wedding-Wind

The wind blew all my wedding-day,
And my wedding-night was the night of the high wind;
And a stable door was banging, again and again,
That he must go and shut it, leaving me
Stupid in candlelight, hearing rain,
Seeing my face in the twisted candlestick,
Yet seeing nothing. When he came back
He said the horses were restless, and I was sad
That any man or beast that night should lack
The happiness I had.

                    Now in the day
All's ravelled under the sun by the wind's blowing.
He has gone to look at the floods, and I
Carry a chipped pail to the chicken-run,
Set it down, and stare. All is the wind
Hunting through clouds and forests, thrashing
My apron and the hanging cloths on the line.

Can it be borne, this bodying-forth by wind
Of joy my actions turn on, like a thread
Carrying beads? Shall I be let to sleep
Now this perpetual morning shares my bed?
Can even death dry up
These new delighted lakes, conclude
Our kneeling as cattle by all-generous waters?

"Wedding-wind", from September 1946, and also designated for
Canto, occupies one page in the Workbook, and the version, as corrected there, is the same as in *XX Poems* and *The Less Deceived*,
except for a few words and some punctuation. There are quite a number of alterations to the single draft, but ten lines of this twenty-three
line poem stand unamended, as first written down. The following reproduces the entire drafting.

The wind blew all my wedding-day
And my wedding-night was the night of the high wind,
And a stable door was banging, again and again,
~~So~~ That he must go and shut it, leaving me
Stupid in candlelight, hearing ~~the~~ rain
                              twisted
Seeing my face ~~twisted~~ in the ~~brass~~-candlestick,
Yet seeing nothing. When he came back
He said the horses were restless, and I was sad
That any man or beast that night should lack
The happiness I had.
                     Now in the morning
                     with
         ravelled   ~~and~~ the ~~blowing of~~ wind's blowing
All's ~~restless~~ under the sun: ~~the wind still blows~~
                         floods
He has gone to look at the ~~fences~~, and I
Carry a chipped pail to the chickenrun,
~~And~~ Set it down, and stare. All is the wind
Hunting through cloud and forests, thrashing
                         clothes on ~~the~~ line
                              the
My apron, and the hanging ~~dancing clothes~~.
Can it be borne, this bodying-forth by wind
         my
Of joy ~~such~~ actions turns on, ~~?~~ like a ~~string~~ thread
~~Of the undreamed joy at the root of the day, and night,~~
   Carrying ~~a~~ beads? Shall I be let to sleep
                         shares

Now this ~~With this~~ perpetual morning~~'s on~~ my bed?
                          fills
~~Will even death conclude~~
Our
~~This kneeling like cattle among new lakes of faith?~~
Can
~~Will~~ even death dry up
These new delighted lakes, conclude
                          by
Our kneeling as cattle ~~among~~ all generous waters?

                              25 [corrected to] 26 Sept

Except for the change of the line "Of the undreamed joy at the root
of the day" — not a bad line in itself — and the rearrangement of the
concluding lines (with the removal of the metaphor "lakes of faith"),
the alterations are largely a "tuning up" of a poem that had arrived.
This is quite astounding in the one poem from *In the Grip of Light*
that is powerful enough to stand beside Larkin's best mature poems.
Once again, the drafting is largely opaque concerning the gestation of
many of the fine lines that make up the poem. As for the impulse to
write this poem of sympathetic identification with a female speaker,
there is no evidence in the Workbook or in the biography, unless,
as Andrew Motion suggests, it reflects one side of Larkin's tortured
ambivalence concerning marriage at the time — an ambivalence that
re-emerged in the slightly later "Sunday Morning".

[Sunday Morning]

Waiting for breakfast, while she brushed her hair,
I looked down at the empty hotel yard
Once meant for coaches. Cobblestones were wet,
But sent no light back to the loaded sky,
Sunk as it was with mist down to the roofs.
Drainpipes and fire-escape climbed up
Past rooms still burning their electric light:
I thought: Featureless morning, featureless night.

Misjudgment: for the stones slept, and the mist
Wandered absolvingly past all it touched,
Yet hung like a stayed breath; the lights burnt on,
Pin-points of undisturbed excitement; beyond the glass
The colourless vial of day painlessly spilled
My world back after a year, my lost lost world
Like a cropping deer strayed near my path again,

Bewaring the mind's least clutch. Turning, I kissed her,
Easily for sheer joy tipping the balance to love.

But, tender visiting,
Fallow as a deer or an unforced field,
How would you have me? Towards your grace
My promises meet and lock and race like rivers,
But only when you choose. Are you jealous of her?
Will you refuse to come till I have sent
Her terribly away, importantly live
Part invalid, part baby, and part saint?

"Sunday Morning", dated 15.xii.47, is seen as the poem that marked the end of Larkin's early "Yeatsian" period. It was written twelve
months after "Thaw", the last poem selected for inclusion in *In the
Grip of Light*; and there are no poems in the Workbook in between.
Larkin himself contended, jokingly, that it "shows the Celtic fever
abated".[5] However, while the poem in part works imagistically in
terms of the realistic setting in which its meditation takes place, turning to metaphor less liberally than did the earlier poems, it shows the
same fluency of composition that had been characteristic of the Workbook so far. This might be construed as indicating that the influence
of "Celtic" ideas about inspiration still lingered. It was not until
"Deceptions" and "At Grass", at the close of the first Workbook in
1949/1950, that we encounter the intense reworking of poems that
was to be a feature of the composition of Larkin's major poems later
in life.

The drafting begins:

Sunday morning

Waiting for breakfast, while she brushed her hair,
　　　　out　　　　　　　empty hotel yard
I looked ~~down~~ at the ~~empty yard's cold enclosure,~~
Once used by coaches. The cobble-stones were wet,
But gave no light back to the loaded sky,
Sunk as it was with mist down to the roofs.
In two rooms electric light was on.
Morning enough for such a sterile night.
But the thought lay crookedly on the stones.
Mortared in sullenness, they were washed clean.
Their whispering filled the courtyard like a mist
You have deserted us, but we remain
Ready outside your life. Morning is poured on us.

Larkin underlined "Mortared" and made a possibly later sardonic note to himself beside it: "They don't use the stuff son!"

Admittedly the poem employs rhyme comparatively little, so that there are few problems of adjustment for it; but this whole passage seems to have come with astonishing fluency: the first five lines, which include only two corrections (one later rejected) are as printed, except that "used" became "meant" and "gave" became "sent", and the definite article before "cobble-stones" is dropped.

In this initial draft, it is the cobblestones that seem to say something to the speaker about his past; and the final conclusion of the poem is too much anticipated in "You have deserted us, but we remain/Ready outside your life." Larkin instead restructured the poem in a manner that was to be characteristic of many of his later poems. The first section was modified so that it presented, in realistic detail, the setting of the emotional confrontation that is to be the heart of the poem, with a tone that is dramatically appropriate to the further development of the poem. This was to be the mode of entry in later poems like "Church Going". The redrafted passage is much as it appears in the printed version. The sequence of end-stopped single-line sentences in the original draft has been removed.

> Waiting for breakfast, while she brushed her hair,
> > down
> I looked ~~out~~ at the empty hotel yard
> Once used by coaches. The cobblestones were wet,
> > sent
> But ~~gave~~ no light back to the loaded sky,
> > > down ~~upon~~ to
> Sunk as it was with mist ~~down~~ the roofs.
> Drainpipes and fireescape climbed up
> Past rooms still burning their electric light:
> I thought: how well the morning suits the night.

Larkin then redrafted the second section, which contained the poem's turning point. This took two attempts, and even the second version was subject to much redrafting:

> Instant regret: for the stones slept, and the mist
> > past
> Wandered absolvingly ~~on~~ all it touched,
> Yet hung like a stayed breath: the lights burned on,
> Pinpoints of infinite excitement: outside the glass
> All that for a year I had not seen

Astonishingly spilled
   ~~Spilled in~~ from a ~~broken~~ merciful vial— my world,
   This tender visiting; again, my world,
To which   meet   ~~raced and~~ like
   My promises ~~met and locked and raced like~~ rivers.
          \once raced/

   Darling
   ⟨~~forced~~⟩

   Misjudgment: for the stones slept, and the mist
   Wandered absolvingly past all it touched,
   Yet hung like a stayed breath: the lights burned on,
   Pinpoints of infinite excitement: beyond the glass
      colourless   day   unbelievably
   The ~~colourless~~ vial of ~~morning mercifully~~ spilled
   My world back after a year
   ~~Spreading my forgotten world~~, my lost, lost world
      cropping   ~~on~~
   Like a ~~fallow~~ deer strayed ~~close to~~ my path again,
           near
   Bewaring the mind's least clutch. Turning, I kissed her,
        sheer
   Easily for / joy tipping the balance to love.

The first four lines are largely the same in both drafts. The metaphor of the "vial" was there at the beginning, though much played about with; but the Yeatsian "fallow deer" (later "cropping deer") emerged only in the second draft. The tension between the realistic opening and the more romantic images of this second section manifests a tension of impulse that Larkin was evidently grappling with at the time.

Once again, Larkin may have had the sense that he was rushing too fast to his conclusion in his first draft, which ended:

          again, my world,
   My promises met and locked and raced like rivers.

This material was in fact moved to the third and concluding section, of which there was only one draft:

   But, tender visiting,
   Fallow as a deer or an unforced field,
   How would you have me? Towards your grace
   My promises meet and lock and race like rivers,

only when you choose.
But ~~first give me your~~ ?— Are you jealous of her?
Will you refuse to come till I have sent
Her terribly away, importantly live
Part invalid, part baby, and part saint?

15.xii.47

This final section was drafted exactly as printed, with only one alteration that gave the phrase "only when you choose". The difficulty in finding how to point a poem to its conclusion, seen in the drafting of the second section of "Sunday Morning", followed by an easy final run, was to be a feature of the drafting of many of Larkin's major poems. Nonetheless, the ease with which the final lines seem to have come, and the readiness not to attempt to modify them, is characteristic of drafting of the earlier work.

It should be said that the drafting of this poem does, in places, show signs of erasure, indicating that aspects of the working are lost to us, and that there may have been more changes than are now evident. This should not, however, undermine the general conclusions concerning it.

"Sunday Morning" marks, as Larkin suggested, a turning point. It was followed by a rather barren period of composition. In those years of the late nineteen-forties, a change was taking place in Larkin's poetry — a change that would be accompanied by a great difference in the drafting of his poems. That change would involve a disappearance of the fluency characteristic of the drafting of his earlier poetry, to be replaced by a more considered manner of composition, in which decisions on minor changes would be the subject of extended trial, and comparatively short poems would take many pages to draft over a period of weeks or even longer.

Chapter 3

A NEW STYLE OF DRAFTING

Larkin said that at the end of 1946 he "gave up the whole business" of writing poetry.[1] In the months that followed, a new influence began to take hold. As Larkin recalled, "I was in some digs which faced east and the sun used to wake me very early in the morning . . . and it happened that I had Hardy's own selection of his poems, and I began to read them and was immediately struck by them . . . by their tunefulness and their feeling, and the sense that here was somebody writing about things I was beginning to feel myself."[2] As he later recalled, "he abandoned the 'Yeatsian properties' of *The North Ship*, and began to find a voice of his own."[3] "Sunday Morning", a transitional poem, and one of the few poems from 1947, shows, as Andrew Motion has pointed out, "the characteristics of both his mentors . . . strongly evident . . . ".[4] The Workbook contains only one poem from 1948, "An April Sunday brings the snow". There is in fact evidence of many pages being torn out of the Workbook at this time; and of this Larkin said, "some missing pages contained material I did not wish to make public, and I probably still have them somewhere; others were torn out simply when I wanted a sheet of blank paper, for any reason."[5] What drafting, if any, is missing we shall probably never know; though one has the impression that the absence of drafts may be due to the fact that this was a difficult period for Larkin, in which he was groping for a way forward.

"An April Sunday brings the snow" was occasioned by the death of Larkin's father, and it is one of Larkin's most memorable early poems. As does much of Hardy's poetry, it gets its emotional power from our normal response to domestic detail. The six poems in the Workbook from the spring of 1949 — "Neurotics" (March–April? 1949), "I am washed upon a rock" (18 March 1949), "On Being Twenty-six" (May 1949), "Modesties" (13 May 1949), "Sinking like sediment through the day" (13 May 1949) and "To Failure" (18 May 1949) — are much less distinguished and perhaps symptomatic of a writer who is trying to find his way in a new idiom - an idiom posssibly epitomized in the first line of the one poem he chose to publish from those years, "Words plain as henbirds' wings" ("Modesties" in *XX Poems*). They

---

The drafting of "Coming" is given in its entirety, but not that of the other poems discussed in this chapter.

are nonetheless important signs of how Larkin was turning away from the Yeatsian ambitions for poetry, to write out of his own strong feeling of the failure of those Romantic ambitions in his own career as poet.

Compositionally, the drafts of these poems are not very interesting: "An April Sunday brings the snow", unfortunately appears in the Workbook only in an uncorrected transcription of its final version. The full working of "Neurotics" is not in the Workbook. What we have follows the final version of "I am washed upon a rock", another poem whose drafting is of little interest: it was arrived at in two pages. The same is true of "Sinking like sediment through the day", where the second page of work is occupied by a fair copy of the final version, this time, unusually, in ink. "To Failure" was the subject of only a page and a half of drafting, evidently on May 17th; and its final version is again a fair copy in ink, made the next day. "Modesties" is slightly more extensively drafted, taking three pages; though, given the simple nature of the poem, the drafting does not reveal a great deal, except that the poem took about as much work as many poems of a similar nature, such as "Toads", took later in Larkin's career. Once again, there is a fair copy in ink. The reason for the ink fair copies of these three consecutive poems is not clear.

"At Grass", completed on 3rd January, 1950, might be seen as the first major mature poem by Larkin; and it brings in a wholly new approach to composition, undoubtedly associated with the abandonment of the inspirational approach to composition associated with his admiration for Yeats, and the discovery, through the influence of Hardy, of the possibility of making poetry out of the things that made up his own life. Talking to John Betjeman on a BBC television programme, he described his early poetry as: "Yeats and water" and remarked that it was "not so much that it is bad, but it was so unreal and without any possible reference to my own life as I was living it";[6] and, while "At Grass" was occasioned by seeing a television documentary, its setting is contemporary. The drafting is much more extensive than that for earlier poems of the same length, with far greater correction of detail than had been encountered before.

At Grass

The eye can hardly pick them out
From the cold shade they shelter in,
Till wind distresses tail and mane;
Then one crops grass, and moves about
— The other seeming to look on —
And stands anonymous again.

Yet fifteen years ago, perhaps
Two dozen distances sufficed
To fable them: faint afternoons
Of Cups and Stakes and Handicaps,
Whereby their names were artificed
To inlay faded, classic Junes —

Silks at the start: against the sky
Numbers and parasols: outside,
Squadrons of empty cars, and heat,
And littered grass: then the long cry
Hanging unhushed till it subside
To stop-press columns on the street.

Do memories plague their ears like flies?
They shake their heads. Dusk brims the shadows.
Summer by summer all stole away,
The starting-gates, the crowds and cries —
All but the unmolesting meadows.
Almanacked, their names live; they

Have slipped their names, and stand at ease,
Or gallop for what must be joy,
And not a fieldglass sees them home,
Or curious stop-watch prophesies:
Only the groom, and the groom's boy,
With bridles in the evening come.

The drafting originally resulted in a poem of nine stanzas, later
reduced to five. The first stanza seems to have come easily:

The eye can hardly pick them out
                              shelter in
From the cold shade they select —
Till wind distresses
To shelter in.   tail and mane:
Then, on the far side of the field,
We see them standing, nose to nose

The first line remained to the end exactly as first written. It em-
bodies both the subject of the poem and its dominant perspective:
the horses are far off, lost to sight, as their past is. Most of the details of the final version are there: the pair of distant horses, standing
close to one another, sheltering in the shade, while the wind disturbs
their hair. After a second draft, Larkin writes out what becomes the
published version of the stanza, except for its final line. There is a
firm sense of the subject and its possibilities implicit in the poem's
opening, quickly come to.

Here, as throughout the drafting of the poem, the rhyming pattern is absent in the first version. This is not to say that Larkin is solely concerned with narrative line or imagery: phrases that carry important feelings for the overall impact of the poem are evolved and retained. When the narrative line shows shape, modifications are made to produce rhymes. In this first stanza, the metrical pattern and the rhyme scheme (a, b, c, a, b, c) for the whole poem are discovered. In addition, other features emerge: "in" and "on" are imperfect rhymes; they have weak natural stress, but are placed in positions where metrically a firm stress is implied. This sets up the natural, muted feel of rhyme and metre that is characteristic of the poem as a whole.

The horses are not revealed to be race horses in the first stanza. That they were famous but now forgotten, becomes the theme of the next stanza attempted:

> Fifteen years ago, they were
> More famous than most men, pursued
> By cameras, field-glasses and cars,
> Ham-sandwiches and newspaper:
>   morning   were
> Their ~~every~~ gallops ~~was~~ reviewed
> By lunchtime in the   spied on from bushes
> ~~In a hundred noisy~~ City bars.   cheered from stands

Larkin redrafted this second stanza, using the original first three lines as the last, to give a new direction to the poem.

> And now no London newspaper
> Prys round their paddock solitude.
> ~~But~~
> They ~~They~~ are as other horses are.
>   both
> Yet, fifteen years ago, ~~they~~ were
> More famous than most men, pursued
>   camera, field-glasses and car.
> By ~~field-glasses and camera.~~
>
> In City dining-rooms, in clubs
> And barber's-shops and billiard halls,
> Their flippant names were burrs that stuck
> To gossip; and in back-street pubs
> Their tinted pictures on the walls
>   every ~~mortal~~ earthly
> Embodied ~~all unearthly~~ luck.

Attention turned to the disturbance of human life produced by the horses as objects of betting — an emphasis taken up again in the fifth and sixth stanzas of the original draft version. We see Larkin trying to plot the direction of the poem beside one rejected version of his original second stanza, where he makes one of his rare notes to himself:

> magic of names — names
> woven into human world —
> names passed into encyclopedias
> — horses, free at last, become
> horses? Do they remember? ?
> the burst of speed

Much of this is taken up later; though the poem was to find its own resolution in slightly different and decidedly more subtle terms. In the meantime, the drafting moved on:

> Through
> ~~In~~ thirty-three and-four, perhaps
>   distances   sufficed
> Two dozen ~~afternoons contain~~
>   fable   far
> To ~~make~~ them, ~~fabled lost~~ afternoons
> Of Cups and Stakes and Handicaps.
>   when   ~~jogged~~ slid by
> ~~Their names, though ours passed on unnoticed,~~
> Now are
> ~~Are now~~ embedded in those Junes,
>
> Parasols and silks
> ~~The silks and parasols~~, mauves and greys —
> What did they make of them?
>   not have been noticed
> Their names, that might ~~have gone unnoticed,~~
> ~~Eternally inlay these Junes~~
> ~~Inlay Now~~ inlay those classic Junes
> Thereby ~~Since~~

There is some groping, as evidenced by the large amount of alteration. When Larkin reaches the phrase that, after two rejected attempts, was to become (with its craft metaphor) "To inlay faded classic Junes", he stops as though he has found what he wanted, and the next version of the stanza is virtually the published one, with "classic Junes" concluding the last line. We see in fact how much the process of composition involves the discovery of phrases or details that at once evoke the world of horses but also carry the emotional movement of the poem.

The next two stanzas attempted to continue the theme of the horses being dominated by human concerns, particularly by money and betting, with lines like "But money rode them, led them in" and "Broke three people in one day". In essaying these stanzas, Larkin at first wrote "They lived in terms of men, hedged in/By bet and bid". Finally eliminated, they were heavily worked over, particularly in the search for the type of everyday detail that was to be a feature of Larkin's poetry from this time on: "A cheaper suit/A better smoke"; "Pawned coats, a week's advance of pay" are among the phrases tried out.

> Broke three people in one day,
> The two between them:
> ~~The two of them; and~~ every race
>   created
> ~~They ran brought~~ small disturbances +
> A pawned ~~topcoat~~ coat ~~a theft~~, an advance of pay
> ~~One pawns his coat, one cannot~~ pay
>   A hundred ~~such~~
> One hunts   ~~tiny~~ humiliations trace
>   to
> Back / their pure-bred energies.

The money/betting theme is reintroduced in the drafting of the last two stanzas, with "pencilled bets" in the penultimate stanza and "Like colts again: they trot for joy/And not for bets" in the final stanza.

> They hang their heads. But this stiff cloth
> Of reputation's slipped their backs,
> ~~And all that tight-sewn~~
> ~~Long since. These~~   ~~are theirs.~~
>   the   odds
> ~~And all the light~~. Twelve years ago: ~~all~~ pencilled ~~bets~~
>   ~~And long since Odds And starting~~
> ~~Long since Bets, Taps, colours, drained away from both~~
>   chattles
>   stable ~~taps~~ had washed up both
> And ~~paddock deserted both~~
>   into
> Their names ~~?~~ the almanacs

The references to betting were eliminated early in the drafting;
and as soon as the phrase concerning "memories" emerged, it was
transformed into its final version "Do memories plague their ears like
flies?", and became the first line of the stanza, thus bringing the
theme of memory into prominence, and returning the poem to the
visual image with which it opened: the scene provides the simile, as
so often in Larkin's mature poetry.

> They shake their heads. Do memories
> Annoy them, now
> And laurelled in the almanacks?
>
> The cloth of gold has slipped their backs.
>
>   ears
> Do memories plague their ~~manes~~ like flies?
>   The dusk comes on.
> They shake their heads. ~~The cloth of fame~~
> Summer by summer, ~~it all dissolved~~ all wore away
> ~~Slipping from their backs fell back~~ away
>   the   —
> The starting gates, ~~and~~ crowds and cries —/
> All but their almanacked names, were all gone, are gone
> ~~Except as names, they were quite forgotten and none~~
> Imagines them

There is reference to the horses trotting like "colts", which brings
back the suggestion, explored earlier, that they will be like other
horses again. The phrase is transformed later to "gallop (if they do)
for joy", and ends up as "gallop for what must be joy". In these
changes, there is a movement away from any presumption to understand the horses' feelings; and the final perspective, as throughout
the published poem, is a human one.

A key metaphor, delicately muted, but given prominence by its
placing across two stanzas is "they//Have slipped their names". It
appears at first as "But this stiff cloth,/Long since slid from their
backs", where the saddle blanket is given a vague, figurative extension. Its suggestions become more specific in "this stiff cloth/Of repu-
tation"; but it is then changed to "The cloth of gold has slipped their
backs", to become "the cloth of fame" in the next draft. It emerges
in a new form as the conclusion to the stanza: "Till the fever and the
money had slipped and gone/From their backs like a stable-cloth".

Finally, as the drafting moves on to the closing stanza, the phrase
becomes a link between the two stanzas, and the metaphor becomes

submerged in "they//Have slipped their names"; while any mone-
tary reference, linking it to the money/betting theme, disappears.
Indeed, Larkin had associated the cloth successively with "reputa-
tion", "gold", and "fame", only to eliminate all of these in favour of
"names", with its more elusive suggestions of his frequent theme of
identity.

"At Grass" is unusual in that, although there is the notation "(fin
3.1.50)" that customarily marks the completion of a poem in Larkin's
workbooks, it did not appear in print in something close to this "finished" form, as did most other poems. There is, indeed, no final
"good version" in the Workbook; but the following is a reconstruc-
tion of what seems to have been the poem as drafted there.

"At Grass"

[Draft version from Workbook — BM Ad MS 52619]
[The stanzas of the published version are indicated by numbers in the
left-hand margin. Changes (other than of punctuation) made in the
published version are shown in the right-hand margin.]

1. The eye can hardly pick them out
   From the cold shade they shelter in,
   Till the wind distresses tail and mane;
   Then one crops grass, and moves about,
   The other seeming to look on.
   The sky blows dark with new Spring rain. /And stands anonymous
                                                          again/

   And now no London newspaper
   Pries round their paddock solitude.
   They are as other horses are.
   Yet, fifteen years ago, both were
   More famous than most men, pursued
   By camera, field-glasses and car.

   In City dining-rooms in clubs
   And barbers'-shops and billiard halls,
   Their flippant names were burrs that stuck
   To gossip; and in back-street pubs
   Their tinted pictures on the walls
   Embodied every earthly luck.

2. Through thirty-three and-four, perhaps   /Yet fifteen years ago,
   Two dozen distances sufficed   perhaps/
   To fable them, far afternoons   /faint afternoons/
   Of Cups and Stakes and Handicaps,

Whereby their names were artificed
To inlay faded, classic Junes.

3. Silks at the start: against the sky
   Numbers and parasols: outside,
   Squadrons of empty cars, and heat,
   And littered grass; then the long cry
   That hangs unhushed till it subside
   To sports editions in the street.   /To stop press columns/

   But money rode them, led them in,
   Curry-combed their croups and flanks;
   Every canter, swerve or sweat
   Money measured; every win
   Was endorsed at different banks.
   Guiltlessly they galloped, yet

   Broke three people in one day,
   The two of them, and every race
   They ran brought small disturbances —
   One pawns his coat, one cannot pay:
   [Strange such seediness to trace]   [Not drafted to completion]
   Back to such splendid energies.

4. Do memories plague their ears like flies?
   They shake their heads. Dusk brims the shadows.
   Summer by summer all ebbed away.   /all stole away/
   — The starting-gates, the crowds and cries
   All but the unmolesting meadows.
   Almanacked, their names live; they

5. Have slipped their names; and stand at ease
   Or gallop for what must be joy.
   No field glasses pursue them home. /And not a field-glass sees them
                                                                home/
   Stopwatches make no prophecies.   /Or curious stop watch
                                                          prophesies/
   Only the groom, or the groom's boy   /and the groom's boy/
   With bridles in the evening come.

Larkin remarked: "It was always my practice to transfer a poem
from manuscript to the typewriter, usually at the point at which a
coherent and consecutive version had emerged; this did not mean that
that version was final. It may be that more changes were made to 'At
Grass' at this stage than is usual . . . "[7] For the published version he
took five of the nine stanzas in his draft, altering some phrases before
the poem appeared in *XX Poems* in April 1951.

These later alterations of phrase are few, and they are noted beside the version given above. In stanza two of the published poem, "Yet, fifteen years ago" is taken from one of the deleted stanzas and substituted, as a linking phrase, for "Through thirty-three and-four". In the third stanza, "stop press columns" is revived from one of the drafts to replace "sports editions"; while "far afternoons" in the same stanza becomes "faint afternoons". At the conclusion, "Only the groom and the groom's boy" rather than "Only the groom or the groom's boy" tidies up the grammar, as the rhyme required the plural "come"; while "No field-glasses pursue them home/Stop watches make no prophecies" is rephrased "And not a field-glass sees them home,/Or curious stop-watch prophesies", presumably to avoid the broken movement at the end of the poem that a series of unlinked clauses would give. Only one alteration seems the work of independent second thought: the "new Spring rain" of the first stanza had been with the poem from the beginning, though "rain" had little emotional function for the poem as a whole. The line now reads "And stands anonymous again", where "anonymous" links forward to the phrase "they//Have slipped their names" in the final stanza, and takes up a note that is in tension with the dominant concern with fame.

The reorganization of the poem for publication can be seen as the final stage in its focusing. The eliminated stanzas have to do with the involvement of the horses in the world of men and the disturbances caused by betting. This theme, which at one stage of the drafting seemed to dominate the poem, does not appear in the published version. Larkin's mode of composition in this poem is completely characteristic of his procedure with major poems throughout the rest of his career. He begins at the beginning, composing line by line, with very few leaps ahead, even to the end of the stanza. It is noteworthy that, as Larkin's stanzas evolve, the thought and narrative line lead the writing, and details and phrases are sometimes developed without regard for the rhyme scheme. This contrasts with the procedures of some poets who employ traditional forms, and who allow the rhyme scheme to suggest the phrasing. We see in all this an early corroboration of the importance of narrative, conscious thought, declarative statement and particular detail in Larkin's work.

"At Grass" was followed by a poem never completed, "Last of all, when a great war has ended". Loosely inserted into the Workbook at this point is a newspaper advertisement for Milletts Army Surplus. Larkin transcribed a list of items from the advertisement, which he intended to use in the poem. This points to his growing and changing interest in everyday things as material of poetry.

"Deceptions" had its origin in another quotation, this time from Mayhew's *London Labour and the London Poor*. Larkin transcribed the quotation in his workbook, but did not immediately begin drafting the poem that it inspired. Between the quotation and the writing of "Deceptions" comes the drafting of "Compline".

Deceptions

'Of course I was drugged, and so heavily I did not regain my consciousness till the next morning. I was horrified to discover that I had been ruined, and for some days I was inconsolable, and cried like a child to be killed or sent back to my aunt.' Mayhew, *London Labour and the London Poor*

Even so distant, I can taste the grief,
Bitter and sharp with stalks, he made you gulp.
The sun's occasional print, the brisk brief
Worry of wheels along the street outside
Where bridal London bows the other way,
And light, unanswerable and tall and wide,
Forbids the scar to heal, and drives
Shame out of hiding. All the unhurried day
Your mind lay open like a drawer of knives.

Slums, years, have buried you. I would not dare
Console you if I could. What can be said,
Except that suffering is exact, but where
Desire takes charge, readings will grow erratic?
For you would hardly care
That you were less deceived, out on that bed,
Than he was, stumbling up the breathless stair
To burst into fulfilment's desolate attic.

"Deceptions", like "At Grass", was subject to far more reworking than were earlier poems; yet we can see in the first page of drafting that a great deal of the final shape is there in the initial working:

Now it's so long ago
Where they ca
Where can they be found,
Even from such a distance I can feel
Even so distant I can taste the grief,
          sharp   made
Bitter and stubly with stalks, he forced you gulp:
                    sun, the brisk, brief
The heartless patterns of -?-

~~Jingle~~ ~~Passing~~ wheels a/ong
~~Rasping~~ ~~Trotting~~ of ~~horses in~~ / the street outside.
      ~~was~~ /triding
All London / ~~walking~~ quickly the other way
 ~~That~~ A/d the ~~daylight~~ greedy
~~And the day~~   ~~?~~   ~~?~~   and unanswerable and wide

Even so distant I can taste the gr/ef,
      ~~?~~
  ~~stalk~~ sharp with stalks /
Bitter and ~~sharp with stalks,~~ /e made you gulp:
    occasional print /
   ~~sun's cold patterns,~~ /nd
The ~~heartless patterns of sun,~~ the brisk brief
Worry of wheels along th/ street outside —
All London walking qui/kly the other way;
      /~~high~~ tall
And light unanswerab/e and ~~wide~~ / and wide
               shame
With nowhere to se/rete the scar, no ~~dark~~
    ~~thirsted for~~
~~You were so thirsty for, no shame, but yours.~~
    / ~~by~~ against
               ~~drawer of knives~~
~~To hide your own against.~~ ~~?~~ ~~drawer of~~
   ~~thoughts lie open~~   ~~drawer~~
~~Your memories glittering like a box of knives~~
     ~~by~~ against
For yours/to hide ~~against~~ by. No concealment drives
Your mi/d lies open like a drawer of knives.

Larkin quickly reaches a striking first line that remains unaltered. His distance from the event, the grief, and the reference to tasting (that is used again) are all in this first line. The images of dazzling light and moving traffic are also there in his first draft: characteristically, they arise from a psychological *observation* — that for those in pain, light seems harsh and the world callously concerned with its own business. The light imagery seems to suggest (or be continued in) "Your memories glittering like a box of knives". When this is changed to the final "Your mind lies open like a drawer of knives", the image of the knives has changed from a visual one to an implicitly tactile and threatening one of sharpness, showing how an image can suggest new possibilities of apprehension.

    Of special note is the second line in the second version, where "sharp with stalks", a phrase from the first version that found its

way into the printed poem, is deleted, only to be replaced before
emendation can take written form. It was not infrequent for Larkin
to work on a phrase, only to return finally to its original.

After correcting his second attempt at this first section of what
was to become a poem of seventeen lines, Larkin already had, in final
form, lines one, two, three, four, six and nine (except for the tense in
line nine); though he was to try a few changes to them (later rejected)
in further drafting.

> Even so distant I can taste the grief,
> Bitter and sharp like stalks, he made you gulp:
> The sun's occasional print, the brisk brief
> Worry of wheels along the street outside —
> All London walking quickly the other way.
> And light unanswerable and tall and wide
> Gives
> ~~With~~ nowhere to secrete the scar, no shame
> against. ─┤   No cover
> For yours to hide ~~by─~~ ~~no concealment~~ shrives.
> Your mind lies open like a drawer of knives.

The pattern of the rhyme and the choice of rhyming words are
almost set: only the rhyming words in lines seven and eight were to
be changed later; and these were to be the lines in the first section on
which he was to expend the most effort in redrafting. They brought
into focus, through images, the girl's attitude to her grief, so crucial
to this first section and to the continuation of the poem. Of the two
rhyming words of these lines, "shame" and "shrive", the second may
have seemed to introduce religious suggestions of absolution that were
out of keeping with the final tenor of the poem. Indeed, the phrases
in which it appears, "no concealment shrives", "No cover shrives",
hardly make sense. The final rhyming words, "day" and "drives", appear in the fourth draft of the first section; though the lines continued
to give trouble through additional drafts. Indeed, the very effective
break in the penultimate line of this first section, bringing a slowing
of movement and an accompanying feeling of coming to an end of
something, appears only later, in the final version in the Workbook:

> out of
> Shame ~~from the~~ shadow.   All the unhurried day
> Your mind lies open like a drawer of knives.

With "unhurried", the contrast between the bright, easy day outside and the agonised feel of the room for the girl is emphasised. The

word "shadows" in the previous phrase was later to be replaced by "hiding", which implies more strongly an active wish to do what is impossible — hide the shame. That change was one of two made after the final workbook version.

The startlingly effective line, "Where bridal London bows the other way", with its suggestion of sanctified sexuality and of ceremony, evoking a world from which the girl has been excluded, went through many attempts, among them:

All London walking quickly the other way;

All ~~cold-eyed~~ virgin ~~swerving~~
~~Where heedless~~ London ~~swerves~~ the other way.
\streaming/

~~maiden~~ bridal bows
Where ~~virgin~~ London ~~looks~~ the other way.

In this last version, "virgin" suggested "maiden", which led on to "bridal"; while the earlier "swerves" had been dropped for "looks", which was then replaced by "bows".

The transition to the second section was not easy. Indeed, even in its final printed form, the poem gives the sense that Larkin was not entirely at ease with the conclusion that he had developed from his evocative opening. The first attempt at the second section comes after three attempts at the first section, when that part of the poem seemed close to completion (though changes already noted were still to be made).

The first lines to be drafted focus attention on the rapist:

he should sweat so
marvel ~~at~~ ~~stumbling~~
I ~~think of his hot stumble~~ up the stairs
To burst into
~~And bursting in~~ fulfillment's [sic] desolate attic.

These lines were not to reappear in the further eight attempts to draft the second section. They re-emerge only in the final workbook version, where they become the last lines of the poem, as in the printed version. It would seem that they appeared to be a misdirection when first written at the commencement of the section; but were later found to provide an appropriate conclusion.

Larkin then attempted a transition that involved an imagined retrospect by the dead girl. After three attempts, this became:

If at this distance, your grave pinched in and lost,
Any part of you keeps going back to that room,
See yourself as I see you, radiant in painful frost;
Radiant because unable to pretend.

"Radiant" signals a reaching for some sense of transcendence in face of the agony and loss that characterise the experience. The gesture is redolent of *In the Grip of Light*, then only months back — the manner from which Larkin was trying to free himself. It is evidence of the strong pull that the Romanticism of that book still had for Larkin, and constitutes another misdirection for the poem. Yet Larkin continued to try to develop these lines through a further five drafts. A "part of you" becomes "your ghost", returning over "the slum of years" that have intervened. The "radiant frost" indeed survives yet another draft, to leave its trace in the penultimate draft in the phrase "pretence is frozen out". Quite apart from their tone, these drafts contain metaphors not drawn from the setting of the poem, in contrast with the poem's final, more effective version that draws a resonance from the actual scene.

"I would not dare console you if I could" emerges on the page before the final draft. It was to appear in the printed version as first written; yet Larkin seems to dicker with the line, writing it out twice more in the half page that follows its first appearance, and then crossing it out, but never altering it. It is only after he has put it behind the phrase "Across the slum of years", so that it is broken by the line end, that he lets it stand. Perhaps this was because it provided him with the rhyming word "dare" that enabled him to fit on the already drafted concluding lines, the first of which ended in "stair".

Across the slum of years I would not dare
                    to be said
Console you if I could. All ~~one can say~~
To suffering ghost or substance is that those
        ~~sharp~~ scald
~~By~~ In   long
~~In~~ that ~~hard frost~~, pretence is frozen out

The "ghost" and the "radiant frost" still linger on, but no longer centre stage. In the final draft, they are gone; and the speaker's poignant dilemma concerning the irrelevance to the dead girl of his feelings makes the matter of the second section:

        have buried
Slums, years,   /   you: I would not dare

Console you if I could. What can be said,
Except that suffering scalds deceit, and where
Illusions scatters, pain is most emphatic?
And you would hardly
~~I do not think you~~ care
                    less deceived
That you were nearer truth, stretched on that bed
                              breathless
                              ~~panting~~
Than he was, stumbling up the ~~eager~~ stair
To burst into
~~And bursting~~ fulfilments [sic] desolate attic.

The date "20/2/50" immediately follows this, indicating that the poem is concluded — or that work has reached the point where the poem can be typed out.

Apart from punctuation, lines one, two, five, six and eight of the second section are as in the printed version, except that "For" replaces "And" in line five, and the commonplace "stretched on that bed" becomes "out on that bed", reemphasising the girl's drugged condition. The rhyme scheme is there, except that "emphatic" was to become "erratic" when lines three and four were redrafted. The phrase "suffering scalds deceit" is not a metaphor that illuminates the relation between "deceit" and "suffering"; though the notion that pain is strongest when illusion is not there to blunt it is clear and cogent enough. What takes the place of lines three and four of this section in the printed version is

Except that suffering is exact, but where
Desire takes charge, readings will grow erratic?

The remarks about suffering have been compressed, and a new observation concerning the effect of desire has been introduced. The phrases "suffering is exact" and "readings will grow erratic" have a clinical quality redolent of the Movement — especially the scientific term "readings" as applied to emotions, and one is tempted to see them as later alterations.

In fact, the conclusion was the subject of revision in Larkin's Workbook No. 2, where the following passage appears, unheralded and without title or date, immediately after the completion of "Wires" on November 4th 1950.

Slums, years, have buried you: I would not dare
Console you if I could. What can be said,

~~always true~~ ~~cheats~~, ~~and~~ is exact, ~~but~~
Except that suffering's ~~never lies~~ but where   ~~and~~ where
     takes over ~~is~~ ~~takes~~ ~~is logging~~ takes over
Desire ~~goes~~   ~~romping~~ ~~measuring~~, readings grow erratic?
For
~~And you~~ would hardly care
That you were less deceived, doped on that bed,
Than he was, stumbling up the breathless stair
To burst into fulfilment's desolate attic.

Coming, as this revision does, after Larkin had written the sardonic "If, My Darling" and "Wants", the tone of the changes is understandable. Perhaps Larkin was readying the poem for inclusion in *XX Poems*, published early in 1951.

These new lines contribute importantly to the emotional stance regarding the girl's suffering that the poem attempts to induce. They not only took a long time to arrive at: they are radically different in tone from Larkin's first attempts, with their "radiant frost". This suggests that Larkin had no clear sense of the development of feeling when he embarked on this portion of the poem, in contrast to the feelings so clearly evoked by the description of the girl's situation in the first section. The question of whether "fulfilment's desolate attic" refers to the act of the rapist or to fulfilment generally is a question that familiarity with Larkin's poetry might make natural. Yet it is not the only aspect of the conclusion of this fine poem that gives unease. The rhetorical disclaimer "you would hardly care" does not quite effectively dominate the effect of the rather academic consolation that is proffered in the conclusion — "you were less deceived". The long drafting, with its eliminations and a final return to the poem at a later date, seems to corroborate the sense that Larkin did not in the end feel secure in the direction in which he took the poem at its conclusion.

Coming

On longer evenings,
Light, chill and yellow,
Bathes the serene
Foreheads of houses.
A thrush sings,
Laurel-surrounded
In the deep bare garden,
Its fresh-peeled voice
Astonishing the brickwork.

It will be spring soon,
It will be spring soon —
And I, whose childhood
Is a forgotten boredom,
Feel like a child
Who comes on a scene
Of adult reconciling,
And can understand nothing
But the unusual laughter,
And starts to be happy.

It should not be assumed that Larkin, after writing "At Grass" and "Deceptions", found himself engaged in extended drafting of all his poems. In the month in which he wrote "Deceptions", "Coming", one of Larkin's early lyrical triumphs, was arrived at very easily, as can be seen from the entire drafting, reproduced below:

<u>February</u>

~~In the evening~~
~~In the evening, in February,~~
~~It is light to leave work~~

~~On longer evenings light is cold and yellow~~

On longer evenings,
Light, chill and yellow
Bathes the ~~the~~ serene
Foreheads of houses.
Laurel-shielded, in
The cold wet garden,
 A
~~The~~ thrush ~~-?-~~ sings,
Astonishing the brickwork.
With a fresh-peeled song.
~~A new sound, fresh peeled~~

On longer evenings,   can understand
Light, chill and yellow,   And ~~understands~~ nothing
Bathes the serene   ~~an~~
Foreheads of houses,   But ~~the~~ the unusual laughter
A thrush sings,   starts
          surrounded   And ~~begins~~ to be happy.
Laurel-~~shielded in~~   25.2.50
     In
The bare deep garden,
Its fresh-peeled voice
Astonishing the brickwork.
It will be spring soon,
It will be spring soon,
And I, whose childhood
Is a forgotten boredom,
Feel like a child
Who comes ~~Who comes~~ on
~~Coming upon~~ a scene
          reconciling
Of adult ~~reconciliation,~~

The second and only full version differs from the first version principally in the rearranging of what had so far been drafted. Some
of the later alterations are minor, affecting only in a small way the
tone or flow of the poem: "Who comes on" for "Coming upon"; "reconciling" for "reconciliation"; "can understand" for "understands";
"starts" for "begins". The only groping was at the beginning of the
drafting, in looking for the first line. The first two lines were originally one. When Larkin sets them out as two shorter lines, he has
found his form and he is away.

"At Grass" and "Deceptions" do, however, mark a major turning
point in Larkin's drafting of his poems. Although there were to be
a few later poems, such as "Dublinesque", that were completed after
little drafting, his major poems, such as "Church Going" and "The
Whitsun Weddings", were to be the subject of intense working of a
kind not encountered before "At Grass".

Chapter 4

THE MOVEMENT POEMS

In 1953, a new tone emerged in British writing: "ironic, intellectual, rigorous, witty"[1] was how it was described in January 1954 by *The Spectator*, which in August hailed the emergence of a new "movement".[2] The works that publicly set the tone of "The Movement", as it came to be called, were John Wain's *Hurry on Down* (1953), Kingsley Amis's *Lucky Jim* (1954) and certain poems by Larkin. One aspect of all these works was that they seemed deflative of received pieties, such as "work" in Larkin's "Toads", perhaps the poem that most seemed to characterise "The Movement" at the time.

"Reasons for Attendance", completed on December 30th 1953, was the first of a series of poems by Larkin that created the new deflationary, sardonic tone. It was also the first poem in which he employed a device that he was to utilise throughout his career — a speaker who emerges as an ironic parody of himself, so that the self-irony has an important influence on the reception of the poem. Other poems of this kind that followed in the next eighteen months were: "I Remember, I Remember"; "Poetry of Departures"; "Toads"; "Places, Loved Ones"; and "Mr. Bleaney".

Reasons for Attendance

The trumpet's voice, loud and authoritative,
Draws me a moment to the lighted glass
To watch the dancers — all under twenty-five —
Shifting intently, face to flushed face,
Solemnly on the beat of happiness.

— Or so I fancy, sensing the smoke and sweat,
The wonderful feel of girls. Why be out here?
But then, why be in there? Sex, yes, but what
Is sex? Surely, to think the lion's share
Of happiness is found by couples — sheer

Inaccuracy, as far as I'm concerned.
What calls me is that lifted, rough-tongued bell
(Art, if you like) whose individual sound

The entire drafting is given of all poems discussed in this chapter.

Insists I too am individual.
It speaks; I hear; others may hear as well,

But not for me, nor I for them; and so
With happiness. Therefore I stay outside,
Believing this; and they maul to and fro,
Believing that; and both are satisfied,
If no one has misjudged himself. Or lied.

The drafting of "Reasons for Attendance" opens awkwardly, as if Larkin were trying to establish a direction and a tone for the poem.

Passing
~~Outside~~ the lighted hall

A trumpet speaking, loud and authoritative,
 ~~Makes me stop dead~~
 ~~Halts me in my tracks~~ aside up
Draws me ~~out of my path up~~
~~Stops me and draws me~~ / to the lighted pane.
I listen a moment. Jazz? No, fooled again.
Just

   voice
A trumpet's ~~speaking~~, loud and authoritative,
~~Drew~~ Diverted me ~~up to~~ towards   glass
~~Draws me aside up to~~ / the lighted ~~pane~~.
 By
~~Through~~ which I saw the dancers shuffling pass

"Jazz? No, fooled again./ Just" is given up, despite its undoubted autobiographical resonance: the fact that the music was not jazz had nothing to do with the direction the poem was to take. The first stanza involves some difficult drafting; but Larkin's first sketch for the second stanza comes easily and is close to the final version. He hits in one go the most telling phrase of the poem, "The wonderful feel of girls"; though he characteristically dickered with the phrase, crossing out "wonderful" in this same draft.

A trumpet's voice, loud and authoritative,
Drew me a moment to the lighted glass
 see the   a crowd
To ~~watch the dancers~~ all under twenty-five—
 Shifting intently, face to flushed face,
~~Shuffling in a composite embrace~~.

~~the beat — they must be happy~~
~~So governed by the music that they seemed~~
~~Its beat expressive~~
 ~~uided~~
~~Governed on to~~ the beat of happiness
Solidly on
      smell of smoke, cosmetics, sweat,
The noise, the ~~smoke, the smell of scent and sweat~~,
The ~~wonderful~~ feel of girls — Why was I outside?
Why were they inside? Sex, of course: but what
Is sex? Simply

The change from "Shuffling in a composite embrace" to "Shuffling intently, face to flushed face" produces a movement that imitates the shifting of the dancers, as the voice is forced to "rearrange" its stance as it moves from one phrase to another. "Solidly on the beat of happiness" has a jazz echo and does not attain the paradoxical force of "Solemnly on the beat of happiness" that later replaced it. The rejoinder to the question "Why was I outside?", which constitutes the beginning of Larkin's argument with himself, was to involve some intense drafting:

A trumpet's voice, loud and authoritative,
Draws me a moment to the lighted glass
   watch   dancers
To ~~see~~ the ~~crowd~~ — all under twenty-five —
Shifting intently, face to flushed face,
~~Intently~~ Solidly on the beat of happiness/

    they ~~seems~~
Or so ~~it~~ ~~seemed~~. Think of the smoke, the sweat,
       out here?
The wonderful feel of girls! Why stay ~~outside~~?
   there
But why are they / inside   yes
  ~~Why go inside, though~~? Sex, ~~of course~~, but what
    ~~The notion, surely,~~ ~~Believing, surely, that~~
Is sex? ~~The thought that happiness~~
  Surely, ~~the notion~~ the notion that
    largest
  to think the ~~biggest~~ share
  in life
Of good / is found by couples — sheer

             it   ~~Fancy~~   I guess
        — Or so ~~they~~ seems. ~~Think of~~ / the smoke, the sweat,
                              ~~wh~~
        The wonderful feel of girls — why stay out here?
But why are   ~~-?- why what takes them inside?~~
  they inside?   takes
         But ~~why then are they there~~? Sex, yes, but what
                      ~~brings~~   ~~-greatest~~ lion's
         Is sex? surely, to think the ~~largest~~ share
              happiness
         Of ~~good in life~~ is found by couples — sheer

         Inaccuracy
         ~~Absurdity~~, as far as I'm concerned.
         ~~What brought me here was art~~, that speaking bell
         ~~And probably some of them~~
  One whose   ~~compulsion~~
           /~~Rough tongued and irresistible I have learned~~
         ~~A~~ What called me here was that rough-languaged bell
                              ~~in~~ spilling ~~its~~ bright sound
         (Art, if you like) ~~that says says we, live -? in ? are interned~~
         ~~Each in himself~~

It is not that Larkin cannot see his way forward: by writing "sheer" as
the final rhyming word of its stanza, he clearly showed that he already
had in mind the striking rhetorical effect of separating the adjective
"sheer" from its noun — first "Absurdity", then "Inaccuracy" — by
the stanza break. What seems to hold him up is getting the right
tone for his side of the argument. "surely to think . . . " seems to
fit the bill; and it is completed, in the second drafting, by "the lion's
share/Of happiness". Once he has got the crucial opening for his
position, Larkin soon finds the antithetical balance of "It speaks, I
hear, others may hear as well,//But not for me, nor I for them".

        Inaccuracy, as far as I'm concerned,
        What called me here was that rough-languaged bell
        (Art, if you like) whose individual sound
        Insists I too am individual —/— .
           It speaks, I hear;
        ~~By pleasing me~~ others may hear as well,

    The startling conclusion is subject to some less than startling at-
tempts:

<pre>
                                  and so
                                  ~~?~~ ~~?~~
But not for me, nor I for them: ~~?~~
With happiness. Therefore I stay outside,
Believing this; and they maul to and fro
                              ~~?~~   ~~partly~~
~~Within~~ Believing that; ~~and both~~   ?   ~~satisfied~~
        me better off   ~~mainly~~
    ?   ~~points out~~
            ~~much superior~~
              ~~the better~~
~~Me, the more gullible, them~~
    ~~easier to gull~~
                            both
                            ~~all~~
                        and ~~both~~ are satisfied
           no one   ~~mistaken~~ ~~sides~~
    If ~~neither~~ has ~~misjudged~~, or lied.
             misjudged himself   29.xii.53
</pre>

He first tries out the comparison of "better off" or "superior"; then the self-irony, typical of him at this period, of "Me the more gullible". The drafting dribbles down until he reaches the celebrated reversal that is to end the poem. Such a reversal had not been encountered in Larkin's poetry before; but turning the poem back on himself or the reader, along with an ironic treatment of the speaker, was to be the strategy of "I Remember, I Remember", "Poetry of Departures", "Toads" and "Mr. Bleaney". These were devices that Larkin must have admired in a poem by his friend, Kingsley Amis, "Something Nasty in the Bookshop", published in *A Frame of Mind* in 1953, and presumably written earlier.

The following day, Larkin made a fair copy of the poem.

<pre>
The trumpet's voice, loud and authoritative,
Draws me a moment to the lighted glass
To watch the dancers — all under twenty-five —
                            to
Shifting intently, face ~~against~~ flushed face,
Solidly on the beat of happiness,

                        smoke
Or so I fancy, sensing the ~~heat~~ and sweat,
                              be
The wonderful feel of girls. Why ~~stay~~ out here?
But, then, why be in there   ~~be in there~~
</pre>

~~should~~
~~Yet~~ ~~But why are they inside?~~ Sex, yes, but what
Is sex? Surely, to think the lion's share
Of happiness is found by couples — sheer

Inaccuracy, as far as I'm concerned.
What called me was that lifted, rough-tongued bell
(Art, if you like), whose individual sound
Insists I too am individual.
It speaks; I hear; others may hear as well,

But not for me, nor I for them; and, so
With happiness. Therefore I stay outside
Believing this; and they maul to and fro,
Believing that; and both are satisfied,
If no one has misjudged himself. Or lied.
                              30.xii.53

He made only three small alterations: "to" for "against" in line 4; "smoke" for "heat" in line 6; and "But, then, why be in there?" for "But why are they inside?" in line 8. On the way, he tried "Yet" for "But", only to reject it. With these alterations, he arrived at the poem as published, apart from punctuation, and with the exception of one word: "Solidly on the beat of happiness" was to be replaced in typescript by the much more effective "Solemnly on the beat of happiness". "Reasons for Attendance" was published in *The Less Deceived* in November, 1955.

Poetry of Departures

Sometimes you hear, fifth-hand,
As epitaph:
He chucked up everything
And just cleared off,
And always the voice will sound
Certain you approve
This audacious, purifying,
Elemental move.

And they are right, I think.
We all hate home
And having to be there:
I detest my room,
Its specially-chosen junk,
The good books, the good bed,
And my life, in perfect order:
So to hear it said

He walked out on the whole crowd
Leaves me flushed and stirred,
Like *Then she undid her dress*
Or *Take that you bastard*;
Surely I can, if he did?
And that helps me stay
Sober and industrious,
But I'd go today,

Yes, swagger the nut-strewn roads,
Crouch in the fo'c'sle
Stubbly with goodness, if
It weren't so artificial,
Such a deliberate step backwards
To create an object:
Books; china; a life
Reprehensibly perfect.

"Poetry of Departures" is one of Larkin's finest poems in the "Movement" manner. It is nonchalantly dismissive of everyday pieties — "We all hate home"; and it confronts the romantic desire to escape from the humdrum with the deflating suggestion that we stay where we are because to escape would only be to take the humdrum with us.

It is one of Larkin's earliest poems to make use of the quoted speech of an imagined second speaker. The first such quoted remark, *"He chucked up everything/And just cleared off"* was possibly the impulse behind the poem, as the drafting begins with that sentence, but set out as a single line, which he changes into two short lines, as in "Coming".

He chucked up everything and just cleared off
~~We whisper within~~
~~My four neat walls whisper the~~

You hear of them, never directly

    — ‿ — ‿ ‿ —
Once or twice I have heard

   ‿ — ‿ — ‿ —
Fifth hand, the epitaph//

   ‿ — ‿ — ‿ —
He chucked up everything,

   ‿ — ‿ —
He just cleared off,

   ‿ — ‿ ‿ — ‿ — ‿
And never without a sneaking

   — ‿‿ —
~~And~~ Envious glow

Here, unusually, there are scansion marks over the whole of the first stanza. Larkin's marking of the four mono-syllabic words, "He just cleared off", with three stressed syllables, gives a hint of why he did this. His ear was remarkably good; but once he found himself writing in short lines where there was an unusual concentration of stressed syllables, he evidently felt a need to examine what he was doing. The short lines are, indeed, redeemed from triteness of movement by the concentration of stresses; and the final result is a poem that reads with a very natural, colloquial pace, despite its being written in eight-line rhyming stanzas with three beats to the line. The effect of natural speech is enhanced by the use of partial rhymes, with the rhyme often falling on an unstressed syllable or syllable of indeterminate stress, as in "epitaph" and "off".

After two further draftings of the first stanza, Larkin moved on to the second.

> Sometimes you hear,
> ~~I've sometimes heard,~~ fifth-hand,
> The epitaph
> He chucked up everything
> And just cleared off,
>   the
> ~~Always said in a~~ reverently
>   ~~Envying~~
> ~~Half afraid voice~~
>   voices
> And the ~~voices would~~ always sound
>   Enviously   ~~obsessed   and~~
> ~~Reverent, and ashamed~~ debased, impressed
>   shameful
>   As if this ~~was the~~ thing
> ~~Everyone~~   \were the/
>   ~~We all~~ wanted most.
>   We all
>
> Sometimes you hear, fifth-hand,
> The epitaph
> He chucked up everything
> And just cleared of,
> And always the voices sound
>   Heartened,
> ~~Envious, and~~ impressed
>   aware
>   ~~conscious   sure they are~~   ~~what~~ they are mentioning
> As if ~~covertly of mentioning~~

    ~~all think the~~   ~~knows to be~~
What ~~we like best~~ ~~Everyone thinks~~ the best
      Is ~~understood as~~
           ~~known to be~~
             agreed as

~~And they are right, I think,~~
~~Everyone hates home~~

And they are right, I think:
Everyone hates home
~~When it turns into~~   And ~~the~~
~~As soon as it is a habit~~   having to be there;
I hate my room
           ~~the~~ Its
  ~~Its pictures~~ ~~And its my~~ quiet tasteful junk
~~Everyone wants to junk~~
         and
Books, records, bed,
And my life in such good order
~~As good as being dead~~

The categorical "Everyone hates home" appears first with the qualification "As soon as it is a habit"; but this qualification is then transformed into a further categorical rejection, "And having to be there".
Similarly, after trying "Everyone wants to junk/Books, records and
beds" he goes back to making "junk" the designation of the contents
of the room. The eliminated line, "As good as being dead", perhaps
makes explicit the background of feeling.

    Larkin then went back to the beginning of the poem to make a
complete draft, dating it "23 Jan 1954", his sign of completion.

    ~~Let's get out of here~~   Poetry of Departures

As ~~near~~ Sometimes you hear, fifth-hand,
  ~~As an~~ The epitaph
        He chucked up everything
        And just cleared off,
      always   will
      And / the voices ~~will~~ ~~always~~ sound
  certain ~~Sure~~
    /~~Certain~~ you approve
        ~~the~~   audacious,
  This ~~Of such an courageous~~ purifying,
    Elemental
~~Primal~~   ~~Ascetic~~ move.

And they are right, I think:
   We all hate
~~Everyone hates~~ home/
And having to be there.
   abhor
— As I ~~resent~~ my room:
    ~~expressive~~ characteristic
Its ~~expressive bits of~~ junk,
               its perfect
Books, records, and bed.   ~~perfect~~   /
(Like   ~~complete good such~~ good order/.
And ~~And~~ my life), ~~in such perfect order~~
    to hear   ~~good~~ ~~such~~
So ~~to hear~~ it said   ~~such good~~
    ~~hearing~~

He walked out on the whole crowd
~~Produces a shiver~~ ~~Makes us all shudder~~
         and
Leaves us flushed / stirred,
   Then
Like / She undid her dress,
Or Take that, you bastard.
      all
We could / do what he did!
    knowing it
And ~~this guarantees~~, stay
    sober
~~Keeps us quiet~~ and industrious,
   I'd do it
But ~~as for me~~ today,
    go

   Jog down the
Yes, —?— nut-strewn roads,
~~Or~~   Crouch in the forecastle
~~Where~~ Stubbly with goodness, if
It weren't so artificial,
Such a deliberate move backwards
    an objecti~~ve~~:
To create ~~a goal~~
Books, china, a life
     ly perfect
~~Notorious for peace~~.
Recognisably

               23 Jan 1954

Some of the corrections were aimed at tightening up the rhythm and increasing the powerful monosyllabic punch: "We all hate home" for "Everyone hates home"; and "Leaves me flushed and stirred" — in every way better than the cliché "Produces a shiver". Both corrections result in clauses consisting entirely of monosyllables. Larkin displays his habit of trying out a correction, only to follow it by a return to the original word: "Sure" for "Certain", with a return to "Certain"; "Like" for "And", with a return to "And". The penultimate line of the second stanza gives an example of sustained chopping and changing. These attempted changes are perhaps a measure of how important nuances of tone and movement are in Larkin's poetry. Certainly, this poem, so sparse in imagery, depends for its force largely on those two features.

Once Larkin had established his manner and direction in the first two stanzas, he composed the second half of the poem relatively easily, though he did not reach the version as we know it. Evidently more changes were made in typescript. "Poetry of Departures" was published in *Poetry and Audience*, 21, on June 10th 1954 and in *Listen*, I, 3 for Winter 1954. It was included in *The Less Deceived*.

Toads

Why should I let the toad *work*
   Squat on my life?
Can't I use my wit as a pitchfork
   And drive the brute off?

Six days of the week it soils
   With its sickening poison —
Just for paying a few bills!
   That's out of proportion.

Lots of folk live on their wits:
   Lecturers, lispers,
Losels, loblolly-men, louts —
   They don't end as paupers;

Lots of folk live up lanes
   With fires in a bucket,
Eat windfalls and tinned sardines —
   They seem to like it.

Their nippers have got bare feet,
   Their unspeakable wives
Are skinny as whippets — and yet
   No one actually *starves*.

Ah, were I courageous enough
    To shout *Stuff your pension!*
But I know, all too well, that's the stuff
    That dreams are made on:

For something sufficiently toad-like
    Squats in me, too;
Its hunkers are heavy as hard luck,
    And cold as snow,

And will never allow me to blarney
    My way to getting
The fame and the girl and the money
    All at one sitting.

I don't say, one bodies the other
    One's spiritual truth;
But I do say it's hard to lose either,
    When you have both.

"Toads" was perhaps the most celebrated poem of the Movement: it confronted the feeling of being trapped for life induced by the current middle-class preoccupation with a secure job, a pension and taking out a twenty-five year mortgage on a home. The entire drafting of the poem occupies only two-and-a-half pages in the Workbook. When asked, "How did you arrive at the image of a toad for work or labour?", Larkin replied "Sheer Genius";[3] and the speed of drafting shows this to have been a little less facetiously dismissive than it might have appeared.

~~How can I tolerate the toad work~~
      ~~upon~~ / only
~~Squatting across my one life?~~

Why should
~~How can~~ I let the toad <u>work</u>
Squat on my life?
Can't I take my wit as a pitch-fork,
And drive the brute off?

           gulp down
Why should I let it ~~tear out~~
    ~~flesh~~ my days' young flesh
~~The rich pulp of my days,~~

                the
        the ~~sour~~ skin ~~and the stone~~ bone
And leave me ~~only the sour skin and the~~
As a supper dish?

~~be content~~   t~~o~~uch my hat
Why should I ~~let it tear out~~
   ~~with~~   ~~its~~   slobbered-on
For   ~~The~~ ──?──?────── ~~day~~ leavings?

/cap
~~Why should I touch my hat~~
~~For slobbered-on leavings?~~

Are mornings a~~n~~d noon ~~a~~ fair swap
   some tatt~~e~~red
For ~~the rags of~~ evenings?

I'll be
   ~~I'm~~ dam~~n~~ed if I~~'ll~~ touch my cap
   For slobbered-on leavings.

Larkin, as usual, arrives almost immediately at his first line in
final form. He also finds, in the first drafting of the first stanza,
both his stanza form and his use of near rhymes — "life"/"off". Yet,
although the poem came very rapidly, Larkin's first attempt at the
poem took him (unusually) in a direction that he abandoned entirely.
The underlying image of what was intended to be the second and third
stanzas is that of the "toad work" disgustingly eating up "the rich
pulp" of his life so that he gets "slobbered on leavings". Additionally,
the attribution to the toad of the power to "tear" was infelicitous.
Larkin concludes his first page of drafting with fragments that were
evidently intended to be used later:

> The stuff that dreams are made on

> And neither causes or symbolises the other
> But I think they're in league.

This outline of his conclusion seems hardly to have rhythm enough
to qualify as verse.

Larkin then took up a new direction. The drafting went even more
rapidly: stanza four was written almost exactly as printed.

Six days of the week it soils,
   ~~an a~~ its   ~~poison~~
With ~~its nasty venom~~ sickening poison, —
Just ~~All~~   ~~Just~~ ~~F~~or paying a few bills ~~—!~~
That's out of proportion.

~~I wouldn't complain~~

                    men
      Lots of chaps live on their wits —
           \folk/   lispers
      (Lecturers, ~~sharpers~~

                                        ~~race~~ loblollymen, louts
                           ~~dealers in musicians,~~ / ~~touts~~
Lazers,   ~~Quiz men, people who deal~~
      Without being paupers;

      Lots of folk live up lanes,
      With a fire in a bucket;
      Eat windfalls and tinned sardines —
      They seem to like it.

      Their nippers have got bare feet,
      Their unspeakable wives
                  ~~midges~~   ~~and and~~
    ~~Are~~ Skinny as / ~~crickets —~~ ~~they~~ yet   whippets are
      No one actually <u>starves</u>.

                        I'd scoff
      Ah, had I the courage, ~~to shout~~
                              But I know all too
                              well that's
      <u>You can stuff your pension:</u> ~~!~~ ~~I well know the~~ the
    ~~Alas, Admirable! But it's the stuff I'm aware~~ it's the stuff
           \~~it's forever~~/
      That dreams are made on:

                  sufficiently toadlike
      For something ~~has squatted in me~~
         squats ~~on its hunkers~~ ~~in me too~~ ~~also~~ in me too
      Has squatted in me
      ~~Within me   a piece of bad luck~~
      ~~On its hunkers, exuding bad luck,~~

      For something sufficiently toadlike
      Squats in me, too;
                  heavy as hard luck
      Its hunkers are ~~cold as a paddock~~
      And
      ~~As~~ cold as snow,

         will never let me
      And ~~I know I shall never~~ blarney
      My way to getting
      The fame and the girl and the money
      All at one sitting.

> bodies
> one ~~shadows~~
> I don't say ~~one's symbol~~ the other
One's ~~A~~ spiritual truth;
> But I do, say it's hard to lose either
> If you have both.

16.3.54

Some of the drafting is fairly routine. He tries out "All" instead of "Just" only to go back to his first choice. The phrase "nasty venom" must have been replaced by "sickening poison" as soon as he had hit on "proportion" as the final rhyming word of the second stanza. His alliterating list of people who live on their wits was evidently an afterthought, as he crosses out his original list almost entirely. The corrections to the two stanzas beginning (in the final version) "Ah, were I courageous enough" are in fact largely a rearrangement of words already there. When he takes up his earlier note for a conclusion, Larkin does not complete the sentence containing the word "symbol" before crossing that word out in evident realisation that it does not fit the tone of the poem.

Perhaps the pace of the drafting was appropriate to the feeling of pace that the final poem gives. The relative ease of writing is characteristic of many of Larkin's poems of a light or satirical kind. The somewhat breezy and colloquial manner is sustained in part by the roughness of metre that goes along with the use of obviously partial rhymes. There is no call for carefully tuned evocative phrasing, as in "At Grass" and the longer poems that were to follow. "Toads" was published in *Listen*, I, 2 for Summer 1954, and was included in *The Less Deceived*.

Mr Bleaney

'This was Mr Bleaney's room. He stayed
The whole time he was at the Bodies, till
They moved him.' Flowered curtains, thin and frayed,
Fall to within five inches of the sill,

Whose window shows a strip of building land,
Tussocky, littered. 'Mr Bleaney took
My bit of garden properly in hand.'
Bed, upright chair, sixty-watt bulb, no hook

Behind the door, no room for books or bags —
'I'll take it.' So it happens that I lie
Where Mr Bleaney lay, and stub my fags
On the same saucer-souvenir, and try

Stuffing my ears with cotton-wool, to drown
The jabbering set he egged her on to buy.
I know his habits — what time he came down,
His preference for sauce to gravy, why

He kept on plugging at the four aways —
Likewise their yearly frame: the Frinton folk
Who put him up for summer holidays,
And Christmas at his sister's house in Stoke.

But if he stood and watched the frigid wind
Tousling the clouds, lay on the fusty bed
Telling himself that this was home, and grinned,
And shivered, without shaking off the dread

That how we live measures our own nature,
And at his age having no more to show
Than one hired box should make him pretty sure
He warranted no better, I don't know.

The same rapidity of composition is encountered in the case of
"Mr. Bleaney". "Mr. Bleaney" was originally called "Lodgers", and
its hero, "Mr. Gridley". In the first draft, the first three stanzas
evidently came easily: with a few changes they became almost as
they are in the printed poem, which has seven stanzas. This is close
to being true of the fourth stanza.

~~Lodgers~~

"This was Mr. Gridley's room. — ~~H~~He stayed
The whole time he was at the Bodies, till
They moved him — " Flowered curtains, thin and frayed,
     to within ~~three~~ five inches of the sill.
Fall ~~several inches short of the~~

        shows a
      ~~looks out over~~ strip of
      ~~looking on~~
The window ~~giving on to~~ / building land
Tussocky, littered. "Mr. Gridley took
My bit of garden properly in hand."
                  no hook
Bed, upright chairs, sixty-watt bulb, ~~I look~~

       no room   bags
Behind, the door, ~~No space~~ for books or ~~luggage~~.

"I'll take it."   that ~~and~~
~~God what~~ So it happens, ~~that~~ I lie
Where Mr. Gridley lay, and stub my fags
On the same ~~souvenir~~ saucer-souvenir, and try

Stuffing my ears with cotton wool to drown
                    ~~devise~~ to buy.
The jabbering set he helped the son ~~construct~~.
                    what time   came
~~The stupid~~ I know ~~how~~ his habits; ~~now:~~ ~~when~~ he / down,
~~What~~   ~~The "flounders"~~ ~~he liked for breakfast~~
~~His liking~~ His preference of sauce to gravy, why

Stephen Regan remarked that "One of the most impressive aspects of 'Mr. Bleaney' is the way in which it utilises a variety of linguistic registers and creates a strong sense of interpersonal speech that cuts across the poem's insistent rhyming quatrains . . . the interaction between [the speaker's] thought patterns and the speech patterns of the landlady creates an impression of dialogue."[4] These effects seem to have been attained with little or no redrafting: the original rhyming words of the first four stanzas remain in the printed version; and the landlady's words remained as first written and in the same positions in relation to the form, except for the change of name from Gridley to Bleaney.

The fifth stanza, concerning Mr. Bleaney's handling of the football pools and the pattern of his holidays, caused more trouble;

~~kept~~   ~~to one~~
~~put~~   ~~backed~~   ~~weekly for~~
~~He always put the same line / in / his pools~~
He ~~sent~~ put the same line weekly in his pools.
~~Three times a week the pictures~~
                    ~~nights~~
~~The pictures three times weekly~~
Deaf in one ear, on Sundays he "lay in".

When Larkin copied out the first five stanzas in continuing his drafting, he made further alterations to this fifth stanza, and redrafted it yet again before going on to attempt the last two summary stanzas. Even then, he was not satisfied; and came back to it after the poem was finished.

Mr. Bleaney

~~Yes,~~   Bleaney
"/This was Mr. ~~Gridley~~'s room. He stayed
The whole time he was at the Bodies, till

They moved him." Flowered curtains, thin and frayed,
Fall within five inches of the sill,

                    land;
Whose window shows a strip of building ~~ground~~
          Bleaney
Tussocky, littered. "Mr. ~~Gridley~~ took
My bit of garden properly in hand."
Bed, upright chair, sixty-watt bulb, no hook

Behind the door, no room for books or bags:
"I'll take it." So it happens that I lie
          Bleaney
Where Mr. ~~Gridley~~ lay, and stub my fags
On the same saucer-souvenir, and try

Stuffing my ears with cotton-wool to drown
The jabbering set he egged her on to buy:
I know his habits — what time he came down,
             for ~~of~~
His preference ~~for~~ sauce to gravy, why

He filled his Pools up just the same each week
~~He put the same line weekly in the Pools,~~
               till the 'Pic' had come —
"Lay in" on Sundays —? ~~his favourite~~ ?
          Oh yes: ~~He spent his holidays at Rhyll parsons were~~
What else? ~~Oh yes.~~ ~~Parsons were hypocrites or fools.~~
~~And~~ Christmas at his sister's house in Brum.

Leeds
Stoke

                       ~~week~~
                  ~~each time~~   ~~the same~~
                  the same each try ~~time~~
He permed the treble chance, ~~the same each week~~
    how he ~~filled~~ ~~spent his holidays~~/
              put his spare time
And ~~the occasional~~ ? ? — the folk
                in
At ~~In~~ Bridlington he lodged with ~~each~~ July,
And Christmas at his sister's house in Stoke/.

The final two stanzas required, in all, three draftings of each of them.

          and watched
But if he stood, ~~watching~~ the tousling wind,
             ~~space~~

~~Hearing the~~ ~~From this unheated room, and thought~~
Out of his lodger's-bedroom window

        stood
      ~~lay~~   tousling
But if he ~~ever~~ ~~stood~~ and watched the wind fusty
  ~~Over~~ ~~Under~~ And   clouds ~~and~~ lay on ~~cold~~ the ~~frowsty~~ ~~bed~~
~~Tousle the~~ ~~?~~ frigid ~~sky~~ from / ~~this unheated box~~, bed
     tried   ~~of it all~~ as himself at
And ~~thought~~ to think ~~of it as~~ / home, and grinned,
And shivered, without shaking off the dread

                  s
    this hired box measured   nature,
That ~~by this dreariness~~   his own richness
~~?~~ Unable to accrete the harvest-show
     grants
Time ~~brings~~ to any but the most meagre

But if he stood and watched the tousling wind
And frigid clouds, lay on the fusty bed
           that this was
Telling himself ~~this was his~~ home, and grinned,
And shivered, without shaking off the dread

That this hired box measured his own nature,
Unable to accrete the harvest-show
Time brings to any but the most meagre
~~Too stingy barren~~ ~~And he would~~
         Too stingy ~~to accrete~~ — fearful to accrete the slow

    how we live measures our
That ~~this hired box measured his~~ own nature
      at his age to have
~~Too~~ And ~~if its by~~ ~~?~~ ~~now he has~~ no more to show
        box ~~then he must be too meagre~~
Than one hired ~~room,~~ ~~he is the more meagre~~ should make him
                 pretty sure
To warrant more, well, that I do not know.

We see some interesting manoeuvring of phrases: "unheated box"
emerged in the drafting of the first of these stanzas in the description
of Mr. Bleaney watching the wind and clouds. It was eliminated, to
reappear as "this hired box" in the final stanza. "But if he stood
and watched the tousling wind/And frigid clouds" survived through
all three drafts; but, evidently, when the poem was transferred to
typescript, the adjectives changed places. Perhaps "frigid wind" had

been avoided as something of a cliché; but the rhythmic incisiveness
of the phrase was more in keeping with the threatening bleakness of
Mr. Bleaney's life as it presented itself to the speaker of the poem.

Of special interest is the original characterisation of what was missing from Mr. Bleaney's situation: "the harvest-show/Time brings
to any but the most meagre". This phrase held its place until the
final draft. Yet, while it may have seemed a way of heightening
Mr. Bleaney's deprivation, there were a number of reasons for ex-
cluding it. In the suggestion that Mr. Bleaney never attained a richness most human beings could expect, it diminished the impact of
Mr. Bleaney's fate by implying that its bleakness was an unusual
fate. In addition, it works not by the realistic presentation of the details of Mr. Bleaney's situation, as does the remainder of the poem,
but by means of metaphor — and a metaphor whose details are drawn
from outside the "universe" of the poem, from the traditional stock
of poetic metaphor.

In the printed version, the extended syntax of the final two stanzas,
where one clause depends concessively on another, has the effect of
bemusing the reader — deliberately one would assume — as to their
full impact, so that the final short, independent sentence, "I don't
know" drops into a prepared situation of puzzlement. The effect seems
one of subtle artistry; and the stanzas were subject to considerable
reworking. Yet the long single sentence was there from the beginning.
The final short, independent, "I don't know", creates the effect of the
speaker himself giving up in puzzlement — an effect not so strongly
achieved in the final manuscript version, where the poem ends "that
I don't know".

The fairly immediate attainment of the felicity of syntax of these
last two stanzas is even overshadowed by the apparent ease with which
so many memorable phrases came in the first writing and remained
unchanged — particularly the sentences attributed to the landlady,
with the placing of their speaker socially through her diction. Perhaps
somebody actually said these things to Larkin: it was certainly the
case, according to Jean Hartley, that Larkin stuffed his ears with
cotton-wool to keep out the sound of the radio in his digs in those
days.[5] These memorable moments of the poem include "took my bit
of garden properly in hand"; "stub my fags/On the same saucer-
souvenir"; "His preference for sauce to gravy"; and they are all there
in the first writing, with no revisions.

When Larkin had completed the drafting of his final stanzas, he
dated the poem "13/5/55", indicating its completion. Six days later,
he returned to the poem to make a new version of the fifth stanza:

> He kept on plugging at the four aways —
> Likewise
> ~~And he~~ their yearly frame: — the Frinton folk
> Who put him up for summer holidays,
> And Christmas at his sister's house in Stoke.

He then dated the poem "19/5/55". Here he finally comes up with the tellingly apt "kept on plugging at the four aways", though there was no hint of this in the earlier drafting. Even "He permed the treble chance", his last previous attempt, did not get the sentence completely in the language of Mr. Bleaney. The rhythmic superiority of the line to any previous attempts is obvious in the way in which it simulates an insistent effort.

This is one of Larkin's most powerful poems; yet it was drafted in three and a half pages, and possibly in one day. Perhaps this is accounted for in part by the fact that he took the fairly simple a/b/a/b rhyme scheme; or perhaps the poem was begun as a lighter, satirical poem and became more tragic as its potentiality revealed itself to Larkin. At one point he tries out the phrase "Too stingy to accrete", possibly indicating an ambivalence or uncertainty in his attitude to Mr. Bleaney's fate.

"Mr. Bleaney" was written after Larkin had sent *The Less Deceived* to the Marvell Press. On the concluding page of its composition, there is what seems to be a draft blurb for the book. The poem appeared in the *Listener* on September 8th 1955, a week before the closing date for subscriptions to *The Less Deceived*. It was not collected until 1964 in *The Whitsun Weddings*.

These lighter poems evidently came much more rapidly than Larkin's longer, more ambitious pieces, causing less concern over attuned felicities of diction or movement, and were written with less exacting rhyme schemes. Nonetheless, the few poems discussed in this chapter, along with the longer and more extensively drafted "Church Going", created a major shift in British poetic taste. Their introduction of demotic speech and deflative strategies into fundamentally unsatiric poems generated a shift in idiom that went along with their assault on "highmindedness", the most notable feature of the Movement for readers of the day. These poems also established what came to be recognised as the distinctive Larkin manner, with their ironically presented *personae* and their deliberate cutting down of expectations, whose saddened recognition nonetheless contributed importantly to the tension of the poems.

Chapter 5

TWO STUDIES IN DISTANCING

Lines on a Young Lady's Photograph Album

At last you yielded up the album, which,
Once open, sent me distracted. All your ages
Matt and glossy on the thick black pages!
Too much confectionery, too rich:
I choke on such nutritious images.

My swivel eye hungers from pose to pose —
In pigtails, clutching a reluctant cat;
Or furred yourself, a sweet girl-graduate;
Or lifting a heavy-headed rose
Beneath a trellis, or in a trilby hat

(Faintly disturbing, that, in several ways) —
From every side you strike at my control,
Not least through these disquieting chaps who loll
At ease about your earlier days:
Not quite your class, I'd say, dear, on the whole.

But o, photography! as no art is,
Faithful and disappointing! that records
Dull days as dull, and hold-it smiles as frauds,
And will not censor blemishes
Like washing-lines, and Hall's-Distemper boards,

But shows the cat as disinclined, and shades
A chin as doubled when it is, what grace
Your candour thus confers upon her face!
How overwhelmingly persuades
That this is a real girl in a real place,

In every sense empirically true!
Or is it just *the past*? Those flowers, that gate,
These misty parks and motors, lacerate
Simply by being over; you
Contract my heart by looking out of date.

Yes, true; but in the end, surely, we cry
Not only at exclusion, but because
It leaves us free to cry. We know *what was*

Won't call on us to justify
Our grief, however hard we yowl across

The gap from eye to page. So I am left
To mourn (without a chance of consequence)
You, balanced on a bike against a fence;
To wonder if you'd spot the theft
Of this one of you bathing; to condense,

In short, a past that no one now can share,
No matter whose your future; calm and dry,
It holds you like a heaven, and you lie
Unvariably lovely there,
Smaller and clearer as the years go by.

"Lines on a Young Lady's Photograph Album" preceded "Reasons for Attendance", and may be regarded as the first of Larkin's "Movement" poems. The deployment of a relaxed, ironic, deflative manner, with a variety of tones or "voices", and embodying the attitudes and speech gestures of the cultural group from which he came, seems to arrive unheralded and without strain. There is no earlier poem quite like it; and the drafting does not give the feeling that he is groping for a new manner. "Lines", along with "Maiden Name", is among the few poems by Larkin occasioned by his relationships with women that can stand beside his best poems. He left behind a large number of poems concerning love, sex and marriage; but many of them seem distastefully simplistic, such as "Self's the Man", or flatly uninteresting, such as "He Hears that his Beloved has become Engaged" — another poem written, like "Lines" and "Maiden Name", in response to the engagement and marriage of Winifred Arnott.

At the time when "Lines" and "Maiden Name" were written, Larkin's affair with the already married Patsy Strang had recently ended. Yet it is Winifred Arnott who inspires the poems. Her departure from Larkin's life through her marriage may have brought on a disturbing questioning of the pattern of his own life — more disturbing than he perhaps might have expected from the nature of the relationship. Whatever the case, the situation was one in which his emotions could evidently be distanced sufficiently for them to be handled with a poised involvement in poems ostensibly playful. In the first poem the emotion of disappointment or loss is handled through a meditation on a photograph album; in the case of the second piece, a poem of considerable intensity and emotional power is constructed about the consequences of a woman changing her name by marriage. In both poems, the ostensibly trivial and commonplace is made to mask, and to give a civilised containment to, emotions that emerge, at least in some of the drafting, as rather rawer than they show in the final poem.

The drafting of "Lines on a Young Lady's Photograph Album" begins:

> At last you yielded up ~~the~~ album, which,
>   like
> Once opened, se~~nt~~ me distracted ~~with~~ a strange chime
> So many days ~~all~~ struck ~~together~~ at the same time

Larkin makes two attempts to complete his first stanza, retaining the figurative "strange chime". When he gets rid of the phrase, the lines begin to fall in place:

> At last you yielded up the album, which,
>   —?—   all
> Once open, sent me distracted. You at ~~every~~ ages
>   at me   the ~~pages~~
> ~~Came~~ Flying ~~up at me~~ from   —?— thick black pages
> Was a gratuity too rich;
>   choked on such nutritious
> ~~Too~~ I ~~foundered among such   —?—~~ images

Larkin then writes out a fair version, makes a few alterations, and attempts the next two stanzas. There is some difficulty with the passage that eventually became "those disquieting chaps who loll/At ease about your early days"; but the same pattern is followed throughout most of the rapid drafting of the first five stanzas, which occupies only three and a half pages: a first draft of a stanza is corrected and then a fair version is written out. The startling stanza beginning "But o, photography!" is written out exactly as printed after only one draft. Indeed, although the poem is a stylistic breakthrough for Larkin, the drafting is extremely fluent and assured.

As frequently with Larkin, the turn of the poem towards its resolution presents difficulty and involves attempts that he later abandons — most notably the reference to making "our futures part of the same scheme":

> ~~And the day had~~
> ~~On a real day a date, and when the shutter clicked~~
>
> ~~On a real day, when I was somewhere else~~
>
> Posed on   else   elsewhere
> ~~Breathing~~ And the day a time that ~~I myself lived through~~!

~~Inside a~~   ~~when I was elsewhere,~~

                  lived, too,
~~Breathing inside a day when I, elsewhere,~~
    was too
~~But But / ignorant and distant.~~
              I lived on
Breathing inside a day ~~when I lived~~ too —
    the
Is that ~~your~~ secret that you are her past

Breathing inside a day I lived on, too ~~+~~
    still
~~So~~ These wet, ~~still~~ parks, these dull quadrangles, seem
  ~~An~~ A
~~Some~~ vivid, instantly-rescinded dream,
   That says
~~So that~~ no matter what I do
                foolproof
  To make the   my own ~~private~~ schemes
~~In future our~~ futures ~~part of the same scheme~~

Larkin then moved into what he evidently intended as his final stanza:

     will keep   /   ~~will be~~
These years ~~will stay~~ forever / closed to me.
      by
By this ~~and~~ not / your beauty
This, not your beauty

After three more attempts, he concludes his drafting with what was to be the last line of the printed version of the poem:

    This is your past that I can never share.
~~So there~~ ~~This will remain however hard I try~~
   ~~Here you will stay,~~ mounted high and dry
    Smaller and clearer as the years go by
    So
~~And~~ I must leave you mounted high and dry
~~Here you~~

         no matter how I try
I cannot join you: you must linger there
Smaller and clearer as the years go by.

This final line was one that had appeared in embryo in the Workbook before "Lines" was attempted. After he had completed "He

Hears that his Beloved has become Engaged" on January 29th 1953, Larkin made some notes to himself, above which were the lines

> Smaller and clearer, the summers,
> Farther and farther away

Between them and "Lines" came the fifteen pages of his abandoned first attempt at writing "Love Songs in Age", a poem evidently about his mother.

A fair version of his final stanza, still using the rather obvious metaphor from photography, was now written out, followed by the date "17.8.53", the usual sign that drafting was concluded and that he was ready to transfer the poem to typescript:

> This is your past that I can never share.
> Developed, fixed and mounted high and dry
> In days I cannot rifle if I try
>   are a
> You ~~stand~~   there
>   stand
> Smaller and clearer as the years go by.

Immediately below, however, comes another version of this stanza, followed by the date "18.8.53". The reference to her loveliness, which intensifies the lyricism into which the conclusion modulates, is introduced.

> There
> Here you are ~~g~~ fixed + mounted high + dry
> In days I cannot rifle if I try,
> For
> So
> ~~And~~
>
> Here I must leave you, mounted high + dry
> In days I cannot rifle if I try,
>   ~~Local and lovely always~~
> ~~But~~ ~~Always locatable and lovely~~ ~~there~~ Always to be lovely there
> Smaller and clearer as the years go by.

Larkin evidently again felt that he had completed the poem to the point that he could transfer it to the typewriter.

This of course is not the poem as we know it. A month later, after writing "Mother, Summer, I" and "At thirty-one", Larkin returned to "Lines". He took up his original penultimate stanza and redrafted it:

                                       on
Standing inside a day I lived ~~in~~ too —
                              flowers
Or is it just <u>the past</u>? Those ~~smiles~~, that gate,
Those misty parks and motors, lacerate
Simply by being over; you
       ~~break~~   looking
Can ~~bruise~~ my heart by ~~being~~ out of date. $+$
       wring

The drafting then took a new direction with the question of why "we
weep/At far off things", and at our "exclusion" from then. Larkin
made an unusual gesture at reassuring himself that what he had written fitted the metre by indicating the scansion. Such marks are rare
in Larkin's workbooks: his ear was too good to need them.

~~And this we know: yet recently I've wondered~~
~~   in the end surely we weep~~
~~That too, but finally we weep~~
~~At far off things because they are it~~

        /   /   /   /   /
That too; but ~~surely~~ in the end, surely, we cry
~~Because we are shut out, yes, but because~~
Not at exclusion, but, being out, because
It's safer now to cry than it ever was

Yes,
   ~~That's~~ true; but in the end, surely, we cry
   Not only at exclusion, but because
It   leaves us
   ~~We are so~~ free to cry. We know <u>what was</u>
     Won't
   ~~Will never~~ call on us to justify
   Our grief, however ~~loud~~ we ~~call~~ across
                     hard   ~~yearn~~
                              yowl
                              ~~howl~~

Once this stanza was in place, he got his next one in final form
immediately, and moved on to his conclusion, which involved a radical
rewriting of his original ending. This also seems to have come fairly
easily:

⎰ The
⎱ This gap from eye to page. So I am left

~~grieve~~
To mourn ~~To feel~~, without a chance of consequence,
    You, balanced on your bike against a fence;
    To wonder if you'd spot the theft
    Of this one of you bathing; to condense,

        ~~a——— that nobody can share~~
In sum, ~~your past which I can never~~ share,
~~No matter whose your future; high and dry~~ to ~~descry~~
    ~~are perceived~~
~~You must remain~~

        no one now
In sum, a past that ~~nobody~~ can share
        ~~you will lie~~ calm and dry
No matter whose your future; ~~on which I feasted, dry,~~
    It holds you like a heaven
~~And~~   ~~you~~; and you lie
Unvariably lovely there,
    and
Smaller/clearer as the years go by.

He again dated the poem, "18.9.53". It is notable that "dry", which began as a quality associated with the mounting of photographs, has moved through the clichéd "high and dry" to become a quality associated with the unspoiled loveliness of the young lady's past.

The well-known lines, "To wonder if you'd spot the theft/Of this one of you bathing", appear for the first time here. There is no attempt at this bit of comic self-portraiture in the earlier drafting of the poem, and nowhere that it might have fitted into the scheme of the first version. However, back in August, when Larkin was working on the penultimate stanza of his first version of the poem, he wrote across the top of the page a note: "hoping you will not see or rather, that you'll see, but not object". This seems to indicate that, when Larkin was bringing his poem to a conclusion for the first time, he saw additional possibilities for it. Yet there may have been other reasons for the return.

The poem, as Larkin had concluded it on September 18th, would have read:

    But shows the cat as disinclined, and shades
    A chin as double when it is, what grace
    Your candour thus bestows upon her face!
    How overwhelmingly persuades
    That this is a real girl in a real place.

Breathing inside a day I lived on too
These wet still parks, these dull quadrangles, seem
A vivid, instantly-rescinded dream,
That says no matter what I do
To make the future my own foolproof scheme

Here is your past that I can never share
Here I must leave you mounted high and dry
In days I cannot rifle if I try,
Always to be lovely there
Smaller and clearer as the days go by.

This might have seemed rather too transparent. The final line of
the penultimate stanza at one point read, "To make our futures part
of the same scheme": this certainly makes the whole passage seem
very revealing; and Larkin's return to the poem may have been out
of a feeling that this was so. In redrafting, he introduced into the
sixth stanza the observation that the past can "lacerate/Simply by
being over". The draft then moves on, with apparent seamlessness,
to explain that "surely, we cry/Not at exclusion, but, being out, be-
cause/It's safer now to cry" —that the past won't "call on us to
justify/Our grief". The rhetorically persuasive "surely", preceding
the statement that "exclusion" is *not* what we cry about, might put
one on guard; and the notion that grief should be justified is an odd
one, for which the poem has done nothing to prepare us. However,
the passage is in keeping with the sense that we are "free to cry";
and this leads into the elegantly turned concluding position that he
is left to mourn the disappearance of things past "without a chance
of consequence". The development of the poem has been contrived
so that the speaker can rejoice in the sense of being "free", even if it
is only "free to mourn" —a position from which the poem can then
segue into its original lyric conclusion.

One change in the final drafting in September of the last stanza—
"nobody can share" for " I can never share" —may seem merely a tuning up, a slight depersonalisation or a generalisation of focus. However, the conjunction in the printed poem of "a past that no one can
share" with "No matter whose your future" suggests that, even if
someone can share her future, they won't be able to share her past,
because nobody can; whereas the conjunction of "a past which I can
never share" with "No matter whose your future" might be read to
imply "I can't share your past, regardless of whether or not I am shut
out of your future": Larkin's own relationship to her future as well as
to her past would have been, albeit subliminally, brought into play.

The point is a tenuous one; and Larkin might have said that the possible implication was just the reason for the change. Yet the first drafting, with its focus on himself, does seem to betray a sadness that he will not be the one to share her future — or certainly that he will no longer share her present. This nostalgic poem, with the distancing strategy of the photograph album, can be seen as a poem about the sad foreclosure of possibilities that the marriage brought for Larkin. The poem is affectionate in a playful manner; and I believe that finding voyeuristic undertones in the ostentatiously "naughty" passage, "wonder if you'd spot the theft/Of this one of you bathing", is misguided. More valid seems an examination of the exaggeration in certain emotive phrases: "strike at my control"; "lacerate"; "Contract my heart"; "we cry"; "yowl". In the context of the playfulness of the poem, the intended effect might be seen as protecting the expressions from being taken wholly seriously. Yet, viewed in the context of the sad and affectionate perspective with which the poem closes, these phrases could be viewed as masking emotion that, more soberly expressed, might seem only too true. They emerge as part of an overall masking strategy in this poem of erotic sadness.

The exploration of such suggestions is a delicate matter, and it might be dangerous to pursue them further. Would it be wide of the poem's impact to see "Faithful and disappointing" as belonging as much to the general stance of the poem as to photography? Or, for those inclined to delve more daringly, what do we say to a poem of erotic nostalgia that begins "At last you yielded up"?

Larkin, rather uncharacteristically, went back to "Lines" three months later on December 28th 1953. He attempted to redraft a stanza and a half, with the following result:

> We know <u>what was</u>
> Never insists we justify
>   the
>   ~~our~~ great oaths that we shout
> Our grief ~~-?   ?   exclaim~~ across
>   ~~despite our promises~~
>   ~~our the oaths we taken~~
>   ~~all~~
> The gap from eye to page. So I am left
>   at ~~this~~ release from
> ~~(Conv~~ Giddy ~~with all this lack of~~ consequence,
>   \such/
> To mourn you, on your bike against a fence;

To wonder dare I risk the theft
Of this one of you bathing: to condense,

We know <u>what was</u>
Never insists we justify
~~these~~
Our grief, despite ~~our~~ ~~the~~ pledges howled across
\all/

~~This~~
This ~~The~~ ~~The~~ gap from eye to page. So I am left,
Giddy at such release from consequence,
To mourn you, on your bike against a fence;
To wonder dare I risk the theft
Of this one of you bathing; to condense,

This redrafting is not reflected in the printed version. It might have been done when he was preparing the poem for inclusion in his *Fantasy Press Pamphlet*, which appeared in March 1954. It does indeed have the appearance of being a version that preceded the final version in the Workbook. Yet, for Larkin to have used a page of a Workbook so much out of sequence would have been very surprising.

Returning twice to the poem, after he thought he had completed it, is not characteristic of Larkin's mode of composition, and it would seem to be symptomatic of an unease concerning his emotional involvement with the subject of the poem. It is nonetheless very characteristic that the portions of the poem to which he returned were the concluding stanzas — the portion of poems that he always found most challenging. The first five of his nine stanzas came quickly and were not subject to additional revision in the Workbook.

"Lines on a Young Lady's Photograph Album" was not the last of Winifred Arnott in the workbooks. Apart from "Maiden Name", the following brief entry occurs:

To
~~On~~ Miss A.W. Arnott
Love you? Why, I'd pay ten quid for you —
Or five, and | another five to get | rid of you.
five to be then
Or five, at least, and five to get rid of you.
then   be

31 Dec '53

Or Ffive, and five more to be rid of you.

　　　　　Darling
Or 　 ? Love? ~~Why,~~ I'd put down ten quid for you:
/ 　five; then five more to be rid of you.

31.xii.53

Love you? Why, dear, I'd pay ten quid for you:
Five down, and five, ~~when I get~~ rid of you.
　　　　　more to get
8.1.54

There is a typescript, entitled "Love", with a slightly different text:

Not love you? Dear, I'd pay ten quid for you;
Five down, and five when I get rid of you.

The occasion is not clear; though the entry follows closely Larkin's last attempt to revise "Lines". The subject evidently preoccupied him at this time.

Maiden Name

Marrying left your maiden name disused.
Its five light sounds no longer mean your face,
Your voice, and all your variants of grace;
For since you were so thankfully confused
By law with someone else, you cannot be
Semantically the same as that young beauty:
It was of her that these two words were used.

Now it's a phrase applicable to no one,
Lying just where you left it, scattered through
Old lists, old programmes, a school prize or two,
Packets of letters tied with tartan ribbon —
Then is it scentless, weightless, strengthless, wholly
Untruthful? Try whispering it slowly.
No, it means you. Or, since you're past and gone,

It means what we feel now about you then:
How beautiful you were, and near, and young,
So vivid, you might still be there among
Those first few days, unfingermarked again.
So your old name shelters our faithfulness,
Instead of losing shape and meaning less
With your depreciating luggage laden.

15 January 1955

"Maiden Name" was completed on January 15th 1955. Like "Lines on a Young Lady's Photograph Album", it is a poem of "wit" in the sense in which this is said of the Metaphysical poetry of the seventeenth century. As with "Lines", a poem of considerable intensity is constructed about a seemingly trivial matter — how we feel about a woman's maiden name after she has married. The drafting occupies seventeen pages in the workbook and involves fairly intensive correction throughout; and this may seem a lot of work for a poem of twenty-one lines that emerges as a delicate and at times playful compliment, as in the lines "since you were so thankfully confused/By law with someone else, you cannot be/Semantically the same as that young beauty".

Although the poem deals obliquely with one of Larkin's persistent concerns, the nature of identity, even in its final version, a submerged rhetoric of love, faith in love, unrequited love, and innocence and defilement can be observed: "wholly/Untruthful"; "you're past and gone"; "How beautiful you were"; "unfingermarked"; "our faithfulness". It is as interesting to stand back from the drafting and note the emergence and supression of the rhetoric as it is to plot the course of composition in a linear manner. The project of writing about the changed relationship with a woman who has just married by focussing on the stange feeling we have about her old name and its reference is perhaps indicative either of a very superficial involvement with the event, or of a need to distance much deeper involvement.

The attempts at developing the third stanza are particularly revealing:

>   dangerously   and
> How ~~clear~~   ~~unaltered! for~~ our love
> Comes flocking
> ~~Flocks back~~ back as if you stood, restored,
>   ~~again behind~~
> ~~Single, unmarked,~~   able as fit
> ~~Once more Again~~   ~~ours~~
> ~~Once more unmarked, ready to be adored~~

Which later become:

> How dangerously unaltered! for our love
> Comes flocking back, as if you stood restored,
> Unfingermarked and fit to be adored.

"Unfingermarked", retained to the end, is odd, suggesting not only "untouched" in a sexual sense, but also the photographs of "Lines" —

an unconscious carry-over. Additionally, the conjunction, "Unfinger-marked and fit to be adored" suggests that being untouched is the qualification for adoration. A still later version of the quoted passage becomes:

> Stationed
> ~~Hanging~~ apart from marriage, calls us home/.
> You as we wanted you are restored,
> Unfingermarked and fit to be adored,
> Made up of all we felt, and all we've come
> To feel we felt.

The phrase "Stationed apart from marriage" rather openly reveals the source of Larkin's preoccupation with the subject of the poem. Later still again, the passage becomes:

> . . . yet it never shone
>
> More brilliantly and distantly than now.
> Nor called our love more confidently home

Elsewhere the name is described as "Dangerous name"; and we encounter the phrase "Yes, you are free of it, but we are not".

The passage "you cannot be/Semantically the same as that young beauty" might have appeared a little above the heads of the public that Larkin venerated in an essay contemporary with the poem, "The Pleasure Principle";[1] though it is in tune with intellectual preoccupations current in his culture group in the middle-fifties. In one drafting of the second stanza, Larkin refers to the maiden name as "A term rejected by its own extension!" "Intension" and "extension" are logical terms referring respectively to the perceived meaning of a term, and to the entities referred to by it; so that the "term", the maiden name, is rejected by the woman, its "extension". The ideas belong to the same logical-empirical philosophical ambience as "a real girl in a real place,//In every sense empirically true!" from "Lines on a Young Lady's Photograph Album"; and they demonstrate how Larkin's poetry is permeated by a sophisticated intellectual awareness at odds with his championing of a poetry that is readily understood. Indeed, one senses that "Maiden Name" in fact makes play with the problem tackled by Bertrand Russell in his famous "Theory of Descriptions", which deals with the logical status of sentences containing phrases like "the present King of France", which are understandable, but have no existent referent.[2]

An earlier reflection on the function of names is to be found in Workbook No. 2, in some drafting from the spring of 1951 that was never followed up:

> Round the circumference are gathered things
> On clear days ~~visible~~ I can see their names
>
> Especially love should have no name
>
> ~~Things gather at the rim of life~~
>
> ~~All things are held in place by names~~
>
>   our
> ~~O decorous names, holding your concepts still!~~
>
> ~~O names, keeping our concepts~~
>
> O names that keep ~~our~~ concepts decorous
> Ensuring they ~~are~~ bearable and untrue!
>
>   decorous
> O names that keep ~~our~~ concepts ~~bearable~~!
> Gathered ~~untruthfully~~
>
>   in place
> O names that keep our concepts safe ~~at bay~~!

The emphasis is on control and distancing — even untruth — whereby the fact that things can be given names protects us and makes experience bearable. In "Maiden Name", the speaker's security seems to be threatened by the withdrawal of the reference the name once had; and Larkin himself said, "maiden names . . . are very powerful things. I often wonder how women survive the transition: if you're called something, you can't be called something else."[3]

As ever, in his drafting of "Maiden Name", Larkin quickly came to the poem's first line. He begins "You'll understand when you are older. Now", evidently intending a stance of someone facing a younger person who cannot understand mature relations between the sexes. He next writes the phrase "Not the long"; and then, below it

> Married, you left your maiden name disused.

The drafting that follows is a recognisable attempt at the poem as we know it. The first line, which sets the cadence of the poem, stayed the same through four draftings of the beginning of the poem, to emerge two pages on, in its final form: "Marrying left your maiden name disused." The scansion was hardly changed by the modification.

The drafting, despite its length, is not marked by any major in-directions — passages that are developed and then abandoned alto-gether. The stanza that took the most drafting was the second one, where the final version has the maiden name "scattered through/Old lists, old programmes, a school prize or two,/Packets of letters tied with tartan ribbon". This list, which might have seemed quite easy to arrive at, was the subject of many attempts by Larkin, who tried out a variety of phrases for places where the lost name would occur: "Sewn in old clothes"; "faded coats"; "envelopes preserved without permission"; "books/Bought to please others"; "hotel registers"; "old attendance-books"; "college theatre programmes". He seems rest-lessly to try out details; and the large number of attempts are not forced on him by the needs of rhyme or rhythm. Sometimes such itemisations come quickly to Larkin; in other cases they take a long time. Yet they seldom involve finding items that have a metaphorical force in the poem as a whole; and this was not so here.

As was frequently the case, when Larkin had his penultimate stanza complete, he quickly completed his final one; though, in this fairly short poem, he was working on all three stanzas early on.

When he dated the poem, the conclusion was not as printed:

>   old   shelters
> So your / name ~~serves~~ our faithfulness
>   ~~year by year~~
> ~~That you otherwise would have in time grown less~~
> Instead of losing shape and meaning less
>   remain
> Till we ~~are quite~~ unmoved, to ~~hear~~ it spoken.
>   hearing
>   15/1/55

These lines were evidently changed in typescript, removing the refer-ence to the devotees still touched by the name whose repetition over the years will slowly come to move them less and less. Once again, in this final change, the involvement of the speaker is further sub-merged. Such a protective submergence seems to have been a feature the drafting of both "Maiden Name" and "Lines on a Young Lady's Photograph Album".

Chapter 6

CHURCH GOING

Church Going

Once I am sure there's nothing going on
I step inside, letting the door thud shut.
Another church: matting, seats, and stone,
And little books; sprawlings of flowers, cut
For Sunday, brownish now; some brass and stuff
Up at the holy end; the small neat organ;
And a tense, musty, unignorable silence,
Brewed God knows how long. Hatless, I take off
My cycle-clips in awkward reverence,

Move forward, run my hand around the font.
From where I stand, the roof looks almost new —
Cleaned, or restored? Someone would know: I don't.
Mounting the lectern, I peruse a few
Hectoring large-scale verses, and pronounce
'Here endeth' much more loudly than I'd meant.
The echoes snigger briefly. Back at the door
I sign the book, donate an Irish sixpence,
Reflect the place was not worth stopping for.

Yet stop I did: in fact I often do,
And always end much at a loss like this,
Wondering what to look for; wondering, too,
When churches fall completely out of use
What we shall turn them into, if we shall keep
A few cathedrals chronically on show,
Their parchment, plate and pyx in locked cases,
And let the rest rent-free to rain and sheep.
Shall we avoid them as unlucky places?

Or, after dark, will dubious women come
To make their children touch a particular stone;
Pick simples for a cancer; or on some
Advised night see walking a dead one?
Power of some sort or other will go on
In games, in riddles, seemingly at random;
But superstition, like belief, must die,

And what remains when disbelief has gone?
Grass, weedy pavement, brambles, buttress, sky,

A shape less recognisable each week,
A purpose more obscure. I wonder who
Will be the last, the very last, to seek
This place for what it was; one of the crew
That tap and jot and know what rood-lofts were?
Some ruin-bibber, randy for antique,
Or Christmas-addict, counting on a whiff
Of gown-and-bands and organ-pipes and myrrh?
Or will he be my representative,

Bored, uninformed, knowing the ghostly silt
Dispersed, yet tending to this cross of ground
Through suburb scrub because it held unspilt
So long and equably what since is found
Only in separation — marriage, and birth,
And death, and thoughts of these — for which was built
This special shell? For, though I've no idea
What this accoutred frowsty barn is worth,
It pleases me to stand in silence here;

A serious house on serious earth it is,
In whose blent air all our compulsions meet,
Are recognised, and robed as destinies.
And that much never can be obsolete,
Since someone will forever be surprising
A hunger in himself to be more serious,
And gravitating with it to this ground,
Which, he once heard, was proper to grow wise in,
If only that so many dead lie round.

28 July 1954

"Church Going", Larkin told John Haffenden, "came from the first time I saw a ruined church in Northern Ireland, and I'd never seen a ruined church before — discarded. It shocked me."[1] The church in the poem is not ruined, or even out of use; and the speaker of the poem hardly sounds shocked; but the experience evidently pointed the direction that the poem was to take. Nonetheless, as will be seen, Larkin had considerable difficulty in finding what to make of the experience in the framework of the poem.

The poem was begun on 24th April, 1954 in Workbook No. 3 and drafted for twenty-one pages. On May 10th Larkin wrote to Patsy Strang that he hoped the poem would "be finished tonight";[2] but, in fact, two weeks later he gave it up, annotating it "abandoned

25/5/54". It was begun again in Workbook No. 4 in the middle of July, after he had worked for some time on a poem about coins ("With time to kill, I sort my change") that was never completed. "Church Going" was then finished, after eight further pages of drafting, on 28th July, making twenty-nine pages of drafting in all.

Larkin on this occasion did not have his opening line when he began. Nevertheless, the line arrives in the first brief page of drafting, where we also see that a sense of what the poem was to be about was there from the beginning:

<del>Repeatedly</del>

<del>Into them, into their weekday silence</del>

<del>I am drawn into their weekday silence</del>

<del>How strange, these dull unattended buildings!</del> <del>numerous</del>

<del>What</del>
<del>Why am I brought repeatedly up and down</del>

<del>What brings me time and again into your silences</del>

<del>Up and down England?</del>

Once I am
<del>First making</del> sure there's nothing "going on"
I steal inside, letting the door thud shud.
   <del>And stand in</del>
<del>Another church.</del> <del>cycle clips.</del>
<del>Take off my</del> <del>remarkable</del> drab
Another church:<del>not a distinguished one</del>
The piles of little books

1-A
2-B
3-A
4-B
5-C[initially D]
6-A
7-D[initially C]
8-C[initially D]
9-D[initially C]

The second shot at a first line, "I am drawn into their weekday silence" names the puzzling experience that will set off the speculations of the poem. Larkin, however, drops this opening, preferring a strategy similar to that in later poems like "The Whitsun Weddings" and "Dockery and Son", which present the speaker dramatically as a version of Larkin himself, who is taken by surprise by the events of the poem. This strategy emerges with the final version of the first line, which comes after six lines of drafting: "Once I am sure there's nothing 'going on'". Elements of the self-irony that are a feature of the opening of the final version are there in this first page of drafting: "letting the door thud shut", along with the "cycle clips". The conclusion of the first part of the poem and prelude to its first "turning point" is also there in embryo: "Another church: not a distinguished one".

Larkin also sets out his rhyme scheme at the head of this first page (though he has to correct the fact that he marked line "5" as "D" before he had used the notation "C"). This reveals a good deal about his mode of composition. Once Larkin has got the material together for the initial stanza, he adjusts it to give him his rhyme scheme. As he proceeds after that, much of the drafting is aimed at fitting the details of the poem to the rhyme scheme (and to the creation of speech rhythms and to the control of diction). The rhyme scheme does not seem to work strongly to *suggest* details or phrasing. Indeed, a good deal of the intensity of drafting arises from Larkin's skill in adjusting the non-aural elements of the poem to fit its aural demands.

In terms of the various structural devices that it brings together, "Church Going" marks a major compositional advance for Larkin. As in his later major poems, such as "The Whitsun Weddings" and "Dockery and Son", he begins with a deceptively unthreatening presentation of the physical details of the situation out of which the emotional tensions of the poem will arise. The speaker of the poem is initially treated ironically, as in other poems from the Movement period; while the stanza form of nine interlocking rhyming iambic pentameters is of a type Larkin was to use in several of his most serious poems in the future.

By the second page, many of the images and phrases of the first two stanzas are there: in particular, the "little books", "sprawling flowers cut/For Sunday", "brass and stuff/Up at the holy end", "the tense, musty, unignorable silence", "Hatless, I take off/My cycle-clips in awkward reverence", "touch the font", "Stare at the roof . . . restored? Someone would know: I don't". The self-deprecatory tone is extended with the denial of any knowledge of church interiors. A slight mis-direction, both in terms of detail and tone, is encountered in a passage, "Catching sight/Of Christ, I turn in some embarrassment"; but this is quickly dropped. After one more draft of the first stanza and two more of the second, the opening is pretty well as in the printed version:

> Once I am sure there's nothing going on
> I step inside/ and let the door thud shut.
> Another church: matting, seats, and stone,
> And little books; sprawlings of flowers, cut
>   ~~brown-edged~~ brownish
> For Sunday, ~~brittle~~ / now; some brass and stuff

                        the
        Up at the holy end; ~~a~~ small neat organ;
                a
        And ~~the~~ tense, musty, unignorable silence,
                    ~~a over years~~
        Brewed [~~for / centuries~~] Hatless, I take off
                ~~since Napoleon~~ God knows how long
        My cycle-clips in awkward reverence,

                . . . .

                . . . .

                                    ~~thick and dusty~~
                            run my hand along the
        Moved forward, ~~slowly~~, ~~touch the / crude~~ / font,
        From where I stand, the roof looks almost new.
        Cleaned, or restored? Someone would know; I don't.
        Mounting the lectern, I peruse a few
                        scale
        Hectoring large-~~type~~ verses, and pronounce
        "Here endeth" ~~+ / /~~ much more loudly than I'd meant:
                    ~~holler~~
~~chuckle~~ The echoes ~~bellow~~ briefly Back at the door
snigger   ~~guffaw~~
                        ~~and~~   ~~them~~   donate
        I sign the book, ~~give them~~   an Irish sixpence,
~~Really~~,
        ~~Reflect~~ the place was not worth stopping for ~~+~~,
        Reflect

The phrase that follows this, "Yet I did stop", at the opening of
the third stanza, immediately establishes itself as a turning point;
but how to go on from there causes Larkin some difficulty. There
are five attempts that begin with that phrase before he finds himself
able to see the way that will take him through to the end of the
stanza. "Wondering what to look for" — a continuation of the self-
irony — is there from the beginning; but the speculation on what
churches will be used for in the future, which is to be the heart of the
poem, does not come immediately. Once again, though, when Larkin
sees the way forward, the physical details come, colourfully and with
the appropriate tone, almost at once — "pyxes", "parchments in glass
cases", "grazed by sheep", "cathedrals as museums" — even though
the exact wording may change later from this second drafting of the
complete stanza:

Yet I did stop: time and again I ~~don't~~,
        ~~some~~
    wasting my time in ~~a~~ ~~cold house~~
And ~~F~~ind myself ~~standing in some~~ / ~~place~~ like this
Wondering what to look for, wondering, too,
When churches fall completely out of use
      ~~do with them~~ into
What we shall ~~use them for~~, if we shall keep
    ~~only~~ \turn them ~~into~~/
Only Cathedrals, ~~open~~
   ~~A few cathedrals~~ as museums/ to show
              ~~their~~
(Plate) their   ~~albs~~, and pyxes   ~~special~~ locked
   their parchments, ~~pyxes~~, ~~albs~~/ in ~~glass~~ cases,
        be ruined
Letting ~~And let~~ the rest ~~go to ruins~~, grazed by sheep,
   Shunned as unlikeable, unlucky places;

Another minor turning point is found at the stanza's end:

    "Shunned as unlikeable, unlucky places".

This points forward, nonetheless, to those who still might come to
the church and to their motives for doing so — and, eventually, to the
speaker himself and his motives. Out of this the details of the next
stanza emerge quickly enough in the initial page of drafting:

And if, in spite of that, people will come
      child
To let their ~~baby~~ touch a particular stone,
    a cancer   on ~~it~~
To wish away ~~an illness~~, or ~~some~~ some
Advised   ~~to~~ walking   ~~special~~
  ~~Traditional~~ night see ~~walk~~ a/ ~~loved one~~ lost one;
   ~~For most~~
  For ~~Beliefs~~ ~~beliefs will lie down side by side,~~
  ~~Like these, and, and Flower/rota, Mrs. Croome~~

     notwithstanding,
  whether, ~~nonetheless~~,   men
And ~~if, in spite of that people~~ / will come
   a
To let ~~their~~ child touch a particular stone,
  charm   chancre
To ~~work~~ away a ~~cancer~~, or on some
        dead
Advised night see walking a ~~lost~~ one.

~~come as long as any~~.
~~I think my kind will be among the last~~
     one
Power of ~~some~~ sort or other will persist
~~Beyond Flower rota: Mrs. Page, Mrs. Croome~~
    ~~draws only~~
~~Although it only draws my kind, for whom~~
     approaches only
Though at the end ~~come only those~~ for whom
  ~~doorless arches~~ weedy floors and arches faintly reek
The ~~arches, windows, weedy floor, still reeks~~,
   an abandoned   ~~some~~ things   ~~missed~~
Like a ~~deserted~~ earth of ~~something lost~~, dispersed
     ~~the broken walls~~   ebbingly
~~Already, psychic cruse, your walls crack~~
~~Already the walls are broken, ebbingly~~
   ~~frail walls~~
The ~~cruse like~~   ~~of the cruse~~
The frail cruse walls helplessly leak

Many of the details in this passage were to stay with the poem: "a child touch a particular stone"; "on some/Advised night see walking a dead one". The second half of the reflection

> Power of one sort or other will persist
> Beyond Flower rota: Mrs. Page, Mrs. Croome

was rather out of key, even if (as is possible) the "flower rota" was something Larkin had actually seen; though "Power of one sort or other will persist" remains as a crucial reflection for the poem. The last lines of this drafting, however, were to constitute an important misdirection in their slightly fanciful (and ultimately conventional) sense that the walls themselves "leak" what is called (on the next page) "invisible wine" — an exuding of what years of ceremonial visitation — "marriage, birth and death" as he finally phrased it — had laid down, "Uniquely undivided". Indeed, Larkin seems here almost to have in mind the ruined church that provided the experience that led to the poem. A redrafting of this passage attempts to develop these less than fortunate figurative features, and introduces a not too happy oxymoron "the stiffened air":

~~Already it escapes, the stiffened air~~
~~Such places breed, the closely-woven wine that here of where~~
   ~~helplessly seeps away the sense atmosphere~~   here
~~Years have laid down~~ // ~~these stone crossroads. where~~

Eventually "the stiffened air" is replaced by "the stiff ghostly silt that men have left". That phrase had a future in the poem, but not at this point.

After certain further misdirections, Larkin found his way to the end of stanza four:

> dubious women
> after dark will ~~silly mothers~~
> ~~motorists~~
> Or; ~~will our children after dark still~~ come
> To make their children touch a particular stone
> To charm a cancer; or on some
> Advised night see walking a dead one?
> will
> Power of some sort or other ~~must~~ go on
> In games, in riddles, seemingly at random; ⫽
> But superstition, like belief, must die,
> ~~when its~~
> ~~And what is left once the old rhymes are gone?~~
> ~~Only the~~
> ~~Only the remnants~~
> ~~What will remain~~
> And what remains/ when disbelief has gone?
> Well, the last visitors may come, as I
> Seeking~~Seeking Drawn by~~ a
> ~~Drawn by~~   has been
> Wanting~~To sniff~~ / the ghostly silt that ~~rains have~~ left
>   a
> By once appointing this ~~their~~ place to pray,
>   year by year
> And ~~to be brought~~ at marriage, birth and deaths
> ~~Giving~~ down   Much   ~~worn~~   slurred
> Writing~~To give their~~ names. ~~Most~~ will be ~~slurred~~ away

The firmness of the writing in the opening lines contrasts with the desultory quality of much of the drafting that surrounds it. We encounter the appearance of one of the key reflections of the poem: "But superstition, like belief, must die", followed by the first appearance of a key question of the poem: "And what remains when disbelief has gone?" The sureness of these phrases is demonstrated by the fact that, once arrived at, they stay in place, unchanged, until the printed version, while many of the details that follow will be dropped or transformed.

Immediately before this, Larkin wrote the line

                                                      (sort
      The last to come may be one of my (kind quality

which represented a reflection that would eventually show the way
to the end of the poem. However, it did not at this moment; and
further indirections occur. Immediately after transcribing stanza four
in near final form, Larkin concludes his page of drafting with two lines
standing alone that suggest a contrast in terms of which he may have
hoped to develop the poem:

      And by the past mean the flower-clustered walls,
                  the green   ~~four~~   anonymous
      And by the dead ~~mean~~ ~~those~~ ~~half-hidden~~ mounds.
                              the

      Meanwhile, the words "And a stiff ghostly silt", were held on to,
as an opening phrase, through a a dozen pages, occurring fourteen
times in all, though usually Larkin got no further than four or five
lines in his drafting. On one of the occasions when he did, one has
the sense of desultory groping:

      And a stiff ghostly silt, as if the shed
      Serious habit of the place lay/round
      Uniquely undivided. How inbred
                              ~~Think~~
      How rare a breathing-space! For ~~For~~ to this ground
       ~~All men~~ People were brought   moments
      ~~Everyone came~~ / at their important ~~times~~
                                  here if at all ~~privately~~
      ~~At~~ (Birth, marriage/ ~~and~~ death); ~~Here~~ they said
         ~~Shall I survive judgement?~~   ~~Lord have mercy~~   ~~upon us~~   ~~here~~
      ~~Soon I shall die~~ /   ~~I am unworthy~~   ~~on me~~; ~~discerned~~
                  ~~change~~
      ~~The creep of time~~
      ~~Change clouding other faces~~

                                  if
      Lord have/mercy upon me; ~~here were told~~   ~~do~~
                              ~~All All these things And~~ such things
      ~~The Earth is a~~ -?- shadow — And ~~these~~ / condense?
      ~~I feel these walls especial~~
                      ~~particular~~   hold?
      Do/walls like this ~~especial~~ ~~shine~~ with a particular dew?
                              run

~~For~~
~~I think their last visitor will~~
      their final visitors   be ~~after~~
I think ~~their final visitor~~ will be ~~wanting~~ wanting
               am
Something like that (perhaps as I ~~do~~); will
Climb the palings, force through clumps

It is significant that these religious meditations do not give Larkin the way forward. He finds the right direction with the lines:

In your blent air all our compulsions touch,
Are recognised, and robed as destinies

These lines, after three more pages, become the opening lines in the drafting of a new stanza, that reaches a full form as:

In your blent air all our compulsions touch,
Are recognised, and robed as destinies.
      future house ~~has stored contained~~ will hold as much
And since no ~~other spot secretes as much~~
         this ~~it~~
The few who fancy ~~this~~ exemplifies
           have ~~have~~ to come
What to be mortal is will ~~seek you out!~~
As I do, hardly knowing why. For such,
      no future space
      ~~in future nowhere~~
And since ~~no future place~~ will house as much
      ~~of what mortal moments~~
~~Of~~ ~~Than ? ? means~~   sediment as you
   ~~Your~~   as you
~~Of this~~ Rich mortal sediment ~~/~~ ~~it is~~, it is
      Still   same
~~To your~~ / over this / threshold ~~still that~~ they will come
~~As I do, trespassing confusedly~~
Trespassing confusedly

In fact, although there is much here that took its place in the conclusion of the poem when it was completed, it was at this point that Larkin abandoned the poem. The opening lines of this stanza, which came almost in the form they have early in the final stanza of the printed poem, still did not lead Larkin to the conclusion he was seeking. Like several other phrases already quoted that were later to find a place in the poem, they had to be repositioned, almost as though Larkin ended up "mining" his previous drafting: "those queer shaped barns" re-emerges as "this accoutred frowsty barn". "Connected somehow with/Where the dead were buried" is the ancestor of the final line "If only that so many dead lie round" — a line that contains an image found earlier as "The green approving mounds we call the dead". The reference to himself "hardly knowing why" offers a suggestion of the final strategy for concluding the poem, but it is not followed up in that way here.

When Larkin returned to the poem in July, it was after extensive drafting of a poem about coins that was never to be published or completed. Towards the bottom of the last page of drafting of this poem he wrote: "a cross of ground/Marking where men came to be serious." The phrase, both in its movement and in what it brings together, seems to contain the elements around which the conclusion of "Church Going" could be structured.

The drafting began once again with the "ghostly silt" — though now "dispersed". Speculation on who will be the last to come to the church as a church leads quickly on to the conclusion of the fifth stanza as we know it:

```
                          who
    Will be the last, the very last, to seek
                        — one of the crew
    This place for what it was — perhaps
    Who tap and jot and know what rood-lofts were?
                        randy
    Perhaps  A ruin-bibber randy for antique7 //
      Christmas-card consultant anxious for
    Or some / romantic        -?-              a whiff
                        and organpipes and myrrh?
    Of gown-and-bands and organpipes and
    Or will it be my representative,

    Led to
    Hurried    Bored, uninformed
```

The opening of this stanza, "A shape less recognisable each week", arrives on the next page.

The crucial question of "who/Will be the last, the very last, to seek/This place for what it was", which links the stanza to the next one, is now developed further:

```
    Bored, uninformed, knowing the ghostly silt
                tending to
    Dispersed, yet feeling for this cross of ground
    Through suburb scrub because it held unspilt
```

Uniquely mixed so much
~~So much now separated~~ now to be found
 Only in separation
~~Separate and~~   — marriage, and birth
And death, and thoughts of these

The "ghostly silt" having finally fallen into its subsidiary place, the
poem moves on rapidly. "Uniquely mixed" along with "marriage and
birth and death" are now brought forward from the earlier drafting to
give "held unspilt/Uniquely mixed so much now found/Only in separation — marriage, and birth/And death", though "So long" replaces
"Uniquely mixed" in the next drafting.

This sixth stanza, as finally drafted, concludes:

                    marriage, and birth,
     And death ~/~ and thoughts of these — for which was built
 This special   for
~~Such~~This / shelter ~~here~~; and ~~other~~ thoughts/on time,
     On being born indigenous to earth
Though ~~And~~ promised faithfully a tearless clime,
     Though if it had, the walls would not be down

However, before Larkin reached this point, yet another misdirection had occurred: "And what if this were true, and what, again,/If it
were not true" began another attempt to develop a concluding stanza.
Larkin starts out nine times with variations on this sentence, before
giving it up. He seems to attempt to associate the church with the
promises that religion had made, and not merely with the cultural
cohesiveness that its ceremonies offered, as he does in the printed
version of the poem. This leads to rather vague gesturing concerning
the impulse and the need to believe:

And whether this is true, and what, again,
If it were not — in short, a serious house
Used for assembling the fates of men/.
I see him pushing into this air by choice
~~Surer than I~~
~~The impulse fired to a belief~~
~~Seeking its dignity~~
~~Not with my instinct~~
          having flowered as if to breathe
(My instinct ~~came to flower~~), ~~simply to ?~~
     complex   strengthen
~~Alone~~ Its ~~complicated dignity could only thicken~~

~~looking~~
~~have~~ ~~thirsty~~   ~~complex~~ ~~balm~~
~~might~~ ~~arrives~~   ~~its~~ ~~complex~~ ~~patina~~
~~As I ? looking for complex dignity~~
As I have, thinking that its complex balm

However, the phrase "a serious house", encountered earlier, now comes back in. When Larkin continues it with the key pair of lines also from earlier drafts, "In whose blent air all our compulsions meet/Are recognised, and robed as destinies", it gives him the way to his conclusion:

A serious house, on serious earth, it is,

                    ~~met~~
In whose blent air all our compulsions meet,
~~Were~~
Are recognised, and robed as destinies, ;
~~So ?   ? , I fancy~~
~~And riding off~~
~~And this respect will not grow obsolete~~
~~And~~   ~~such~~ ~~this~~   ~~can~~
As ~~this~~ / it never will be obsolete
    ~~? to my~~
                       will
   ~~can~~   n   ~~can~~
And / that much ~~never~~ ~~can~~ be obsolete
   ~~While~~
~~?   ?   ?   ?~~
       ~~anyone~~
~~As long as ?~~
    ~~someone~~
Since ~~there will~~ someone will forever be surprising
  ~~private~~
A / hunger ~~in himself~~ for a place like this,

A serious house, on serious earth, it is
In whose blent air all our compulsions meet,
Are recognised and robed as destinies.
And that much never will be obsolete,
Since someone will forever be surprising
                 to be more
~~Within himself~~   ~~something~~ serious,
A hunger in himself ~~for such as this~~
~~And for a start will circle to this ground~~
~~And drifting And still astonished~~

therefore ông
~~For no~~ And / gravitati~~ng~~ ~~towards~~ ~~to~~ this ground
~~That~~ As ~~being the~~
      fit   to growi~~ng~~ wise in
Reputedly a place ~~for~~   ~~if only for the reason~~
  ~~That he has heard dead folk~~
                ~~all~~
If only ~~that dead people~~ lie around.
   that so many dead

           28/7/54

The drafting of this poem, whose argument finally seems so natural and relaxed, had been difficult, and Larkin had found himself groping as he tried to focus his attitude to what the Church had stood for and to its passing. When the drafting was completed, there remained in many stanzas phrases that did not appear in the printed version of the poem; and Larkin, as usual, did not write out a completed version. As was his custom, he evidently transferred the poem to the typewriter, assembling his version as he typed it out, and no doubt making final changes. No typescript of the poem survives. "Church Going" was sent to *The Spectator*, who lost the typescript for a year, finally printing it on 18th November 1955, more than fifteen months after its completion in the Workbook, and in the same month as the publication of *The Less Deceived*, in which the poem appeared.

Even then, the pieces had not fallen completely into place. The version in *The Spectator* had, in the penultimate stanza, "And death, and thoughts of these — round which was built/This special shell?" — phrasing that must have reflected Larkin's original typescript. This version of the poem was printed in *New Lines* in 1956. *The Less Deceived* originally had "for whom was built" — grammatically unsatisfactory, and evidently a misprint, not corrected until the edition of January 1962; though the mistake was repeated in the first paperback edition of 1973. The misprint is followed in many anthologies. On the *Listen* recording of *The Less Deceived*, made in 1958, Larkin read "for which was built"; and *Collected Poems* follows this. This is what Larkin had drafted in the Workbook; and it seems that we now have the poem as he intended it.

Chapter 7

THE WHITSUN WEDDINGS

The Whitsun Weddings

That Whitsun, I was late getting away:
    Not till about
One-twenty on the sunlit Saturday
Did my three-quarters-empty train pull out,
All windows down, all cushions hot, all sense
Of being in a hurry gone. We ran
Behind the backs of houses, crossed a street
Of blinding windscreens, smelt the fish-dock; thence
The river's level drifting breadth began,
Where sky and Lincolnshire and water meet.

All afternoon, through the tall heat that slept
    For miles inland,
A slow and stopping curve southwards we kept.
Wide farms went by, short-shadowed cattle, and
Canals with floatings of industrial froth;
A hothouse flashed uniquely: hedges dipped
And rose: and now and then a smell of grass
Displaced the reek of buttoned carriage-cloth
Until the next town, new and nondescript,
Approached with acres of dismantled cars.

At first, I didn't notice what a noise
    The weddings made
Each station that we stopped at: sun destroys
The interest of what's happening in the shade,
And down the long cool platforms whoops and skirls
I took for porters larking with the mails,
And went on reading. Once we started, though,
We passed them, grinning and pomaded, girls
In parodies of fashion, heels and veils,
All posed irresolutely, watching us go,

As if out on the end of an event
    Waving goodbye
To something that survived it. Struck, I leant
More promptly out next time, more curiously,
And saw it all again in different terms:

The fathers with broad belts under their suits
And seamy foreheads; mothers loud and fat;
An uncle shouting smut; and then the perms,
The nylon gloves and jewellery-substitutes,
The lemons, mauves, and olive-ochres that

Marked off the girls unreally from the rest.
      Yes, from cafés
And banquet-halls up yards, and bunting-dressed
Coach-party annexes, the wedding-days
Were coming to an end. All down the line
Fresh couples climbed aboard: the rest stood round;
The last confetti and advice were thrown,
And, as we moved, each face seemed to define
Just what it saw departing: children frowned
At something dull; fathers had never known

Success so huge and wholly farcical;
      The women shared
The secret like a happy funeral;
While girls, gripping their handbags tighter, stared
At a religious wounding. Free at last,
And loaded with the sum of all they saw,
We hurried towards London, shuffling gouts of steam.
Now fields were building-plots, and poplars cast
Long shadows over major roads, and for
Some fifty minutes, that in time would seem

Just long enough to settle hats and say
      I nearly died,
A dozen marriages got under way.
They watched the landscape, sitting side by side
— An Odeon went past, a cooling tower,
And someone running up to bowl — and none
Thought of the others they would never meet
Or how their lives would all contain this hour.
I thought of London spread out in the sun,
Its postal districts packed like squares of wheat:

There we were aimed. And as we raced across
      Bright knots of rail
Past standing Pullmans, walls of blackened moss
Came close, and it was nearly done, this frail
Travelling coincidence; and what it held
Stood ready to be loosed with all the power
That being changed can give. We slowed again,
And as the tightened brakes took hold, there swelled

A sense of falling, like an arrow-shower
Sent out of sight, somewhere becoming rain.

Larkin gave the following account of the composition of "The Whitsun Weddings": "I began it sometime in the summer of 1957. After three pages, I dropped it for another poem that in fact was finished but never published. I picked it up again, in March 1958, and worked on it till October, when it was finished. But when I look at the diary that I was keeping at the time, I see that the kind of incident it describes happened in July 1955! So in all, it took over three years".[1] The diary was destroyed after his death. The poem that intervened was "Letter to a Friend about Girls", begun on 16th October 1957. He returned to "The Whitsun Weddings" on 16th March 1958 and worked on it mainly in May and June. After another twenty-three pages of drafting in Workbook No. 4 up to 6th September, he continued on 19th September in Workbook No. 5, which had previously been used for an autobiographical sketch dating from the 1940s and for poems from November 1953 and January 1955. He completed his drafting on 18th October 1958, after a further eight pages, making thirty-four pages in all for this poem of eighty lines, which had taken over a year to compose.

He gave the following account of the experience behind the poem: "You couldn't be on that train without feeling the young lives all starting off, and that just for a moment you were touching them. Doncaster, Retford, Grantham, Newark, Peterborough, and at every station more wedding parties. It was wonderful, a marvellous afternoon."[2]

As often with Larkin's poems, the drafting begins with a memorable line that remained unchanged as the first line of the poem: "That Whitsun I was late getting away". Equally characteristic is the fact that Larkin crossed it out and tried another version: "Why was I late that year getting away", which he also deleted before drafting commenced again with the original first line. However, Larkin continued to play with the largely irrelevant question of why he was late getting away — "From pique"; "Perhaps from chance"; "(My fault, no doubt)"; "Something must have stopped me getting away" — until the fourth draft of this first stanza, when things came into place and the near final version of the stanza is reached.

> That Whitsun I was late getting away
> ~~Not till~~
> It was ~~almost~~ about

                    glistening
                    ~~sunlit~~
One-twenty on the ~~brilliant~~ Saturday
Did   ed
~~That~~ ~~When~~ my three-quarters-empty train pulled out,
All windows down, all cushions hot, all sense
Of being in a hurry gone.   We ran
Behind the backs of houses, crossed a street
Of blinding windscreens, smelt the fishdock: thence
The river's level drifting breadth began,
Where sky and Lincolnshire and water meet.

            slowly
     Running / south
     ~~All afternoon~~   in that long ~~traversing~~ curve

            in a long southwards curve
                    ~~line~~
All afternoon ~~the track bent slowly south~~

It was at this point, after Larkin had set out the first stanza and
attempted to move into the second, that he left the poem for "Letter
to a Friend about Girls". When he returned, the next seven pages
of drafting, which took place from March into May, were expended
on the second stanza. The "sun" or "heat" — the "tall heat" of the
final version — was there from the start, and yielded an opening that
it might have seemed a shame to reject:

Taller than trees, deliberate weight of sun
      Slept on the land.
The sheep were scattered with their shadows: none
Did more than lift a narrow head and stand
      ~~the~~ a
Unmoving in ~~a~~ mist of seeding grass,
                    over
As harmless steam shook out ~~above~~ their backs
                    As
                    ~~Then~~
To fade beyond them. ~~Soon~~ they fell behind
                    opened
The river drew away, and ~~open~~ glass
                    ~~?~~   ~~shone~~ glistened
Of market gardens ~~?~~ ~~glinted, and~~ our tracks
~~Followed~~ Fell in a wide curve
~~Bent~~   ~~slowly with~~ south, all afternoon

The search for appropriate detail took Larkin in many directions, with consequent intense redrafting:

```
                    The river soon
        Fell            and roofs Houses A town
Sank Sank out of sight,/ and sheds began to pass;
  ?            Rubbish and
  ?        Between them, recreation grounds:  Our tracks
        Fell            by
Followed held in a wide curve south all afternoon.,
        went shining throughout and
        And Mile after mile of         all
        Through the heat all England, looked the same
            switched off, relaxed
        Open to summer like a garden frame
```

Larkin made seventeen attempts in all to get into this stanza before he was satisfied enough with the drafting to pass on to the next stanza. Some of the attempts lasted only one or a few lines:

```
All afternoon the blue sky stayed the same.
    The tall heat slept.
England stood open like a garden frame
As past its pane-bloomed distances we kept
                through along canals   lanes
A slow curve south, alongside links  and farms
                        games      seas
Past cooling-towers and cricket-grounds and seas
Of
```

These "cooling-towers" went out, as did the "cricket-games", only to reemerge memorably towards the conclusion of the poem. The "sheep . . . scattered with their shadows . . ./Unmoving in a mist of seeding grass" eventually gave way to "short-shadowed cattle". The "river" that "soon/Sank out of sight" indeed disappeared from view; as did "Rubbish and recreation grounds". The "garden frame" simile became a realistic detail: "A hothouse flashed uniquely". Changes to the first lines resulted in

```
All afternoon, through the tall heat that slept
    For miles inland
```

—the final version, in which "tall" is (Audenesqely) applied directly to "heat". These lines and the next two or three were themselves the subject of ten attempts before Larkin could draft through to the end of the stanza. By then the details had changed; and the "hothouse", the "Canals with floatings of industrial froth" and the "dismantled cars" had arrived.

In contrast, the opening of the third stanza came immediately, almost as in the final version:

> But much less quickly noticed was the noise
>   The weddings made
> Each station that we stopped at: sun destroys
> All interest for what's happening in the shade,
>   And down the long cool platform whoops and skirls
>   ~~Could~~
> That ~~Might~~ have been porters larking with the mails

(I have been told that Larkin once said that this last line contained a private joke concerning a girl named Porter, who had rejected his attentions, along with a play on his own name and on "mails"/"males". Such ingenuity would not have been out of character.)[3]

What was it that delayed Larkin so long with the images in the second stanza? They are highly evocative of a train journey on a hot Saturday in England in the mid-nineteen-fifties; and many of them are recognisable as features of the journey from Hull to London in those days. A feeling of richness and density in a landscape of pastoral ease is evoked; and this is no doubt dramatically appropriate to the poem. This may be seen as reaching forward to the "postal districts packed like squares of wheat"; and it functions as a setting that comes to contain what disconcerts the speaker who seems initially at ease, as in poems such as "Dockery and Son". Yet one might ask what "floatings of industrial froth" or a "hothouse" that "flashed uniquely" or "dismantled cars" have to do with weddings? It could be said that they are in keeping with the ironies exploited in the physical details of the weddings. However, there is not a handling of detail and situation so that it is at the same time realistic and metaphorical, as in some of the poems of Edward Thomas. The orchestration of images produces what one might call a "novelistic" evocation of setting.

The details of the wedding parties, heavily toned with social and class indicators, are also novelistic, with a Betjemanesque flavour. In this case, many of them came in a first drafting in final form and stayed:

> As if out on the end of the event
>   Waving goodbye   ~~While~~
>   when
>   all that would   ~~So~~ I ~~lent~~ leant
>   To ~~something that~~ survived it. ~~As~~ they went

                        swam
        a second   drew
    To watch another lot went past, and I
  Could see the thing them all   in different terms—
        Saw the whole thing again enough to grasp
                        broad
    The fathers with their workmen's belts under their suits
                    mothers worse than fat,
    And seamy foreheads, anxious to be off
An   The uncle
        Uncles is shouting smut, and then the perms
            nylon gloves and
    The costume jewellery jewellery-substitutes,
    The lemons, mauves and olive-ochres, that

    Marked the Marked off the
    Marked off unreal girls unreal girls unreally from the rest.
        Since they alone

More difficult was the characterisation of the attitudes of the various
members of the weddings, particularly the attitude of the girls, for
which various phrases— "Something they could not solve", "easily
forget" — are tried out:

                And who could
                    tried to to guess
                \no one/
    By looking at their faces, what it was
    Reflected in   Children found it dull.
                        not at
    Now going from them/ Kids helped least of all
        To   clearly watched it was all
    The fathers, seemed to watch / a great success
                        \huge/
    That made them laugh; the mothers saw it as
    A kind of secret happy funeral/,

                their handbags
    And The girls, stood, gripping sought there
        The girls ?   tightly gripped discovered seemed to see
            something so /-? stood ?
            snatching a   ?
                                had
    And girls, their handbags tightly-gripped, their smiles
                    hesitant
            Grown strange and lean

```
                                          stared hard a scene
And  But                                  discussed
     And girls, their handbags tightly gripped, could see just stared
     At seeing go  They could not solve
     However long they stared  /Nor
   Something they could not solve easily forget/, that might have been
              difficult         as to
   A joy so new and clear  it might involve
        worse        and yet be envied
   A deeper pain, yet still
```

With the latter part of the fifth stanza and much of the sixth in disarray, Larkin, on June 16th, wrote out a version of the poem from its beginning. Once the fifth stanza was reached, its conclusion and the transition to the sixth stanza — the parts that concern the attitudes of the different members of the wedding parties — took a further three and a half pages of drafting over a period extending from June into July.

However, once Larkin turned to the description of the journey to London, the physical images came easily, so that, at only the second attempt, these lines, in all their felicity, are more or less as they were in the final version:

```
        Free at last
                  what all
     And loaded with the sum of all they saw,
     We hurried towards London, shuffling gouts of steam.
   Now Fields became land was
Here   Now fields were / building-plots, and poplars cast
                              as more
     Long shadows over major roads, and for that  ?
   The postal districts  ?  closer
     The last half hour   our  round us

     Now fields were building-plots, and poplars cast
     Long shadows over major roads
```

In the drafting of the seventh and penultimate stanza, we encounter one of the major indirections of the poem. After the evocative dramatisation of voice in the first lines — "Just long enough to settle hats and say/I nearly died" — the poem moved to a contemplation of the futures that awaited the various couples:

```
     Just long enough to settle hats and blow say
        I nearly died
        Confetti-clear  I nearly died
```

~~All down the line train~~
~~The couples down the train began~~
      ~~lives~~
    ~~married live~~ got under way
A dozen ~~marriages set of in line~~
    marriages
Some had lived far apart, some side by side;
    meant what they
Some ~~had told lies~~ had promised but would lapse
               ~~but on~~ but on
~~One pair this time would never set up house arrive at all~~
~~Some would be dead next year~~
But on   ~~The twilit~~
    ~~But on the bottomless sea bed~~
    One pair within a week would set up house
~~Under~~ ~~Beneath~~   sea
Beneath ~~On the sea's~~ half-lit ~~bed~~, in seventy years
    Another pair would meet the press, perhaps
    Describe their wedding ~~day~~. — and

Larkin is clearly groping for a resolution of the poem, and follows this direction through four drafts. Finally, he abandons it and turns to a description of what is seen from the train on its journey into London, reviving two images from earlier in the drafting: "Against the sky, the cooling towers, the view/Of someone running up to bowl". However, as the stanza began to firm up towards its final version, Larkin stopped drafting on September 6th, possibly at a loss as to how to conclude the poem — or possibly for a purely practical reason, such as preparation for the beginning of term at Hull.

When Larkin came back to the poem after another two weeks, he worked on the penultimate stanza, and four days later had it in near final form — though it would undergo considerable tinkering before completion:

Just long enough to settle hats and say
    I nearly died
A dozen marriages got under way.
They watched the landscape, sitting side by side:
An Odeon went past, a cooling tower,
                  ~~and none~~ though
And someone running up to bowl: ~~and none~~   none
    ~~Of the different couples down the train would~~
~~Thought though the rest and they would never meet~~
    Yet all their lives would ~~have this common~~ be the same this
And yet ~~Their lives would all contain this common hour~~:   hour

                         spread out
        I thought of London ~~lying in the~~ in the sun, ,
                         packed like
        Its postal districts, ~~thick as~~ fields of wheat,/

Larkin had originally written "The postal districts spread out in the
heat", but moved to the image of "fields of wheat", suggestive of
fertility. This association of the "postal districts" with fertility and
love is oddly encountered in a poem from February or March 1951,
never completed, "Two by two in February air". It contains the
lines "Today let love be treated as a joke/Unloose the little loves to
fly in pairs/About the postal districts". The lines in "The Whitsun
Weddings" may be an unconscious recollection, if anything.

    Finding a conclusion that would *complete* what had gone before
was harder:

                    evening fall of endless
        There   ~~endless~~
    ~~Here~~ as the ~~settled particles of~~ dust
            Enriched the light
            ~~Came settling down~~
            ~~settling~~
    In ~~endless~~ ~~endless particles of dust~~
    ~~To make it evening~~
    Under the evening's
    ~~There, as the evening fall of endless dust~~:
            ~~There we were aimed~~
            ~~Enriched the light~~
                            enhancing
    Under the endless light ~~enriching~~ dust
            N~~o~~w of settling du
            ~~There fell~~   Evening brought down:
    There/we were aimed, there we should scatter, just

    There we were aimed, there we should separate

            They wd be lost in the coming populous fields

The passage, "There, as the evening fall of endless dust/Enriched
the light", is one of the most lovely in the drafting; and Larkin may
have been reluctant to see it go from the poem. The "enhancing
dust" —one version from this passage— belongs to a family of images
to which Larkin was drawn throughout his life in moments where the
promise of transcendence tempted. He begins, too, to make attempts
to play with further conventional figurative suggestions of fertility,

"scattering" and "separation" and "dividing", which carry associations with seeds, made explicit in "wandering like seeds". Here the approach to the images is as a metaphorical projection of the theme of the poem, in contrast with the handling of detail elsewhere in the poem. Finally, however, Larkin rejects these images and goes, as earlier, to images that are associated realistically with London main-line stations of the day (in this case, King's Cross). "The knots of rails" appear and "soot mossed walls", with working "men" who "stood up" as the train passed; and finally the "standing Pullmans". None of these, except the "knots of rails", has a metaphorical function for the poem as a whole; though the evocation of the conclusion of the journey — the major metaphor of the poem as a whole — with "raced across" and "tightened brakes" has a powerful and complex figurative effect. Finally, Larkin finds the "arrow-shower" and its association with "rain".

At the bottom of the page on which Larkin finds that image, he sets out what appears to be one of his few notes to himself: "Running edge between the past + future". This evidently indicates that he intends to end in a way that points from this present moment to a future. He does this in his conclusion, which is in a manner he came to favour in other of his longer poems — with the "sand-clouds" in "Dockery and Son" and the "peak" in "The Old Fools": he introduces a metaphor that is not derived from the setting of the poem, but belongs to the traditional store of natural metaphors, here an "arrow-shower" becoming "rain". He told Jean Hartley that the image was suggested by memories of the Olivier film of *Henry V*, which he must have seen in the nineteen-forties.[4] There the shower of arrows from the British bowmen is focused on independently before it reaches its target — one of the memorable images of the film — associated there with victory, but also with death. In Larkin's use, the killing aspect of arrows is subdued, though the sense of "aim" is strongly felt.

When Larkin dated the poem "18.10.58" as concluded, the final stanza, as corrected, is not quite as in the printed version:

> There we were aimed. And as we raced across
>   Bright knots of rail
> Past standing Pullmans, walls of blackened moss
> Drew
> ~~Came~~ close, and it was nearly done, this frail
>   what   held
> Travelling coincidence: and ~~all~~ it ~~bore~~
>   ~~Would be turned loose scatter free on London~~
> ~~Was ready to be loosed on London.~~ There ~~and be changed~~

~~To drift and lodge and~~
    ~~imminent~~ ~~ready~~ to be loosed
Stood ~~ready to be cast at London~~ with all the power
    ~~eager~~ ready
That being changed can give. We slowed again
                               came
    And as the tightened brakes took hold, there swelled
~~This time for good~~
         falling like an arrow-shower
A sense of ~~arrows falling in a shower~~
~~That drops~~
    ~~Dropping from~~
    ~~Far out of~~ sight, somewhere turning to rain.
Sent out of
                 18.10.58

We see, in fact, how much "tuning up" had still to be done when he took the poem to the typewriter. There exist two typescripts of the poem.[5] The variations between them and the final version are few, and mainly ones of punctuation; though Larkin stayed with "turning to rain", rather than the "becoming rain" of the printed version.

The imagery and its development in the poem reveal much about Larkin's art. The railway journey, of course, operates as a major underlying metaphor, full of rich implications for the marriages in its coming together and moving towards a destination. The images of detail, as has been suggested, do not on the whole operate in a metaphorical way to support the feelings evoked by the weddings; and there is little evidence in the drafting of any attempt to make them do so. Setting and situation are evoked in a realist manner, often metonymically: "An Odeon went past, a cooling tower,/And someone running up to bowl". This is the manner of the opening, where Larkin works a long time to draft the second stanza, so evocative of the England from which the marriages will come, and from which they derive a depth and significance; but having figuratively little to do with marriages. Only a few images, such as the "postal districts packed like squares of wheat" ("meant to make the postal districts seem rich and fruitful" as Larkin put it[6]) and the "tightened brakes" are at once part of the actual scene and a metaphorical enhancement, leading to the final metaphor of the "arrow-shower", not derived from the setting. Indeed, in his reading of this poem, Larkin seems to emphasise, by a change of voice, the special status of this final metaphor.[7]

This runs contrary to the way in which poetry was read, and, by implication written, in the period in which the poem was composed. Images were employed (or examined) for their instrumentality in enhancing the theme of a poem, often metaphorically. Larkin broke with this. The structuring of the poem, with its heavy development of setting and incident, is novelistic. As Andrew Motion put it: "It combines a discursive, novel-ish spread with the emotional intensity of a lyric".[8] Larkin told John Haffenden that the poem was "just the transcription of a very happy afternoon. I didn't change a thing, it was just there to be written down"; and went on to say "It only needed writing down. Anybody could have done it".[9] But not anybody did. The remark was made late in Larkin's life, when he tended to make such aggressively simplistic statements about his art. The contention that he "didn't change a thing" may seem odd concerning a poem that took a year and thirty-four pages of drafting to complete. No doubt Larkin had in mind that all his efforts were directed towards being true to the experience. As he remarked on the recording of *The Whitsun Weddings*:

> Looking at "The Whitsun Weddings", the poem from which this collection takes its name, makes me realise that, while in some poems the work you have to do, the effort you have to put in, goes towards following up the original gift, the original few words, the original vision, and seeing where it leads, finding out its natural development; in this poem the work all had to go into recreating the whole experience which came all at once, and which, as it built up slowly through the afternoon, I knew could be a poem, if only I could be fortunate enough to transcribe it.[10]

Though this still implies a rather uncomplicated conception of the way in which the author's sense of things and his relationship to his medium enter into any written characterisation of experience, especially in the case of an author so explicitly and implicitly judgemental as Larkin, the notion of the poem as transcription points up the realist bent of his writing.

Chapter 8

CHANGING DIRECTION

Dockery and Son

'Dockery was junior to you,
Wasn't he?' said the Dean. 'His son's here now.'
Death-suited, visitant, I nod. 'And do
You keep in touch with —' Or remember how
Black-gowned, unbreakfasted, and still half-tight
We used to stand before that desk, to give
'Our version' of 'these incidents last night'?
I try the door of where I used to live:

Locked. The lawn spreads dazzlingly wide.
A known bell chimes. I catch my train, ignored.
Canal and clouds and colleges subside
Slowly from view. But Dockery, good Lord,
Anyone up today must have been born
In '43, when I was twenty-one.
If he was younger, did he get this son
At nineteen, twenty? Was he that withdrawn

High-collared public-schoolboy, sharing rooms
With Cartwright who was killed? Well, it just shows
How much . . . How little . . . Yawning, I suppose
I fell asleep, waking at the fumes
And furnace-glares of Sheffield, where I changed,
And ate an awful pie, and walked along
The platform to its end to see the ranged
Joining and parting lines reflect a strong

Unhindered moon. To have no son, no wife,
No house or land still seemed quite natural.
Only a numbness registered the shock
Of finding out how much had gone of life,
How widely from the others. Dockery, now:
Only nineteen, he must have taken stock
Of what he wanted, and been capable
Of . . . No, that's not the difference: rather, how

The entire drafting of "The Explosion" is given, but not that of the other
poems discussed in this chapter.

Convinced he was he should be added to!
Why did he think adding meant increase?
To me it was dilution. Where do these
Innate assumptions come from? Not from what
We think truest, or most want to do:
Those warp tight-shut, like doors. They're more a style
Our lives bring with them: habit for a while,
Suddenly they harden into all we've got

And how we got it; looked back on, they rear
Like sand-clouds, thick and close, embodying
For Dockery a son, for me nothing,
Nothing with all a son's harsh patronage.
Life is first boredom, then fear.
Whether or not we use it, it goes,
And leaves what something hidden from us chose,
And age, and then the only end of age.

"Dockery and Son" is a poem in which there seems to be very little distance between the speaker of the poem and its author. It is a poem that moves forward with a clear sense of direction. It was begun on February 4th 1963; but it looks back to a visit Larkin made to his old college at Oxford, St. John's, on the way back to Hull after attending the funeral of his predecessor as Librarian, Agnes Cuming, a year before.[1] The idea of the poem may have been with him since the visit, as its first line appears across the top of a page in the Workbook dated "13.5.62", immediately after the completion of "Wild Oats". The line appears above an unfinished poem that had the projected title, "Under a Cloud", work on which evidently led into the drafting of "Essential Beauty":

> would have been   wouldn't
> "Dockery ~~was~~ junior to you, ~~wasn't~~ he?
>   We've got his son here now."

The line was possibly prompted by a memory of a phrase from Julian Hall's *The Senior Commoner*, a novel about life at Eton, which had excited Larkin when he discovered it while still at school, and about which he wrote an essay, "The Traffic in the Distance", in 1982. There he quoted a passage that contains the lines, "Junior to you, am I? But you've got a boy or a grandson or something at the place now. I haven't. I haven't got anybody."[2]

Work on "Dockery and Son" began on February 4th, 1963. The phrase, "Dockery was junior to you", opens the drafting, as it opens the final version of the poem, along with the Dean's other remark,

"His son's here now". At first this is followed immediately by "I started calculating how . . . Dockery . . . /Could possibly have"; but Larkin began again, filling out his opening to include the recollection of how he once stood in the same room twenty years before to give "our version" of what took place "last night". The next day Larkin began work by retranscribing the first stanza, achieving the final version except for one phrase, "Dark-suited, visiting". After writing four lines of his second stanza, Larkin started drafting it again, and arrived, following corrections, at a version close to the final one. The speed of composition is remarkable: the natural, colloquial flow of "But Dockery, good lord:/Anyone up today must have been born/In '43, when I was twenty-one . . . " came without correction.

The articulation of the characteristics of the young Dockery and the transition forward from what he had already written caused Larkin some trouble; but again he moved very rapidly when he reached the narrative of the train journey:

<pre>
                               sharing rooms
And board-faced pub̷l̷i̷c̷-schoolboy I ~~suppose~~
With Cartwright w̷h̷ó was killed?
~~I held a door for once or passed the bread?~~Well, now and then
nudges   ~~one gets j̷olts~~
Life ~~gives~~ ~~Life gives these jolts to anyone who assumes~~

~~And board-faced public-schoolboy, sharing rooms~~
~~With Cartwright, who was killed? Well, now and then~~
                   ~~anyone~~
~~Life drops and catches any everyone, just when~~

And board-faced public schoolboy, sharing rooms
                              ~~it just shows~~
~~With Cartwright, who was killed? Well, that's my fault~~
~~Not everyone does nothing, I suppose~~

   White collared
   ~~board-faced~~
~~And here am I.~~ public-schoolboy, sharing rooms
                           Well, it just shows
With Cartwright, who was killed? ~~Think of my life~~
How much . . . how little . . . Yawning, I suppose
             at
I fell asleep, ~~not~~ waking ~~till~~ the fumes
      glare
And furnace-~~fires~~ of Sheffield, where I changed,
And ate an awful pie, and walked along
</pre>

>   and watched
>   ~~and beyond the roof~~ to the end   ~~to see~~
> The platform ~~till the roof~~   ~~and saw~~ the ranged
>   reflect~~ing~~ ~~the~~   a
> Joining and parting lines, ~~and thought how~~ strong
>
> Unhindered moon. To have no son, no wife,   ["wife" over "heir"]
>   still seems quite natural
> No house or land ~~while Dockery has all four~~

"Cartwright who was killed" has been slipped in — one of the many
casual details that have a larger resonance in the poem as a whole,
such as finding the door to his old room "Locked". Cartwright is another contemporary who had a different fate — that of being deprived
by an early death of the chance of choosing a future. After halting at
the transition more than once, Larkin moves forward in one go with
the dramatisation of himself as tired and not knowing what to think:
"Well, it just shows/How much . . . how little . . . Yawning, I sup-
pose/I fell asleep". The key image of the "Joining and parting lines"
is achieved without correction. Then comes what seems a marvellous
piece of serendipity. The phrase "and thought how strong" already
implied a continuation of the sense over the stanza break. Larkin corrects the phrase to "reflect a strong", which has a much greater sense
of incompleteness: "strong" is no longer a part of an adverbial phrase,
but is an adjective standing free of its noun, which must follow in the
first line of the next stanza. In fact, it is separated from another adjective, "Unhindered". The phrasing "strong//Unhindered moon" has
the effect of making the words "strong" and "unhindered" stand out
with a degree of separation that gives them a wider resonance, suggesting a quality that the speaker perhaps missed in the development
of his own fate, which is the central theme of the poem. The effect is
heightened by the conjunction with the phrase "ranged/Joining and
parting lines", where the separation of "ranged" and "Joining" over
the line end enacts what is pictured.

On February 10th Larkin transcribed his drafting so far, and gave
the poem its title, "Dockery and Son"; though he set beside it an
alternative, "For Dockery & Son". He also set out the rhyme pattern
for the stanzas on which he was working, including the penultimate
stanza. The rhyme scheme was evidently not intended to be quite the
same for any two stanzas. This was not in fact followed; and, in the
final version, the last two stanzas do have the same rhyme pattern.

One of his few new corrections in the first three stanzas was the
substitution of "Death-suited, visitant" for "Dark-suited, visiting" —

a change that was to remain with the poem. "Visitant" seems superior to "visiting", in that it attributes a quality to Larkin rather than describing an action he is performing. "Death-suited", however, seems idiomatically unfortunate. The occasion of the visit to Oxford had been a funeral; but this is the only phrase in which that event impinges on the poem, while the biographical fact has no relevance for the completed poem and is not revealed by it. Many events in the poem have a figurative significance, such as the "ranged/Joining and parting lines" that suggest the various intertwining fates; but such details are presented in realistic terms and take on a figurative sense in the context of the poem as a whole. "Death-suited" instead substitutes a metaphor for a description; and, even if comprehended without the extraneous knowledge of the funeral, must either seem decorative or else must carry with it a figurative effect something like "dressed for death" or "headed for the grave, like all of us". It belongs more to the idiom of poems like Dylan Thomas's "Twenty-four years" than to the realist idiom of "Dockery and Son". One senses that Larkin, in transcribing this part of the poem, may have felt that "Dark suited" did little for the poem, however biographically true it might have been; but it was by that time too entrenched in the metrical structure to be merely removed.

When Larkin came to articulate the differences between his attitudes and those of Dockery, he again had difficulty. This, after all, is the nub of the poem. He returned to this part of the poem six days later, on February 16th:

<pre>
                        an   ⌠This was one
         This was just one more   │ more encounter
                    instance of the   ⌡ with the

         Unhindered moon. To have no son, no wife,
              and so on
         No house or land still seemed quite natural.
This was another instance of, there comes   the
         Every so often, though, you get this shock
Every so often, though, there comes that shock with
         Of finding out how far you've gone in life,
                              \I'd/
         How widely from the others. Dockery, now,
         Think Only nineteen, yet he had taken stock
         Of what he wanted and was capable
                        quite   rather it's rather it's
         Of . . . No, it's not quite that: consider / how
                    that's not the puzzle
                         difference
</pre>

~~Convinced he was he should be added to~~
He knew already adding meant increase.
       ~~meant~~ was   ~~Where do~~   ~~So it goes~~
To me it ~~was~~ dilution. ~~There you are~~ ~~There you are~~
     ideas come from? where ~~do these ones like these~~
~~Where do we get ideas like that~~

In an attempt at these last lines the week before, Larkin had written:

Convinced he was he should be added to.
People are like that. Often you can't see
Where they leave off and where their wife, their two
Delightful kiddies and the rest begin.
~~I don't dilute~~

Convinced he should be added to
That

The notion that Dockery could not be distinguished from the "wife" and "kiddies" that made up his fate was now dropped in favour of "Where do we get ideas like that", which posed the question that was to be the heart of the poem. However, when Larkin continued with his drafting of these lines on 16th, he changed his question, to ask another one that he was later to include in "Aubade" — "Why does it take/So long to see the uncorrected swerve":

Convinced he should be added to.
He knew already adding meant increase.
               Why does it take
To me it was dilution. ~~Where do they come from~~
        the
So long to see ~~what~~ uncorrected swerve
We're sent with into life?

In making the change he introduced a metaphor "uncorrected swerve", which was not to survive in the poem. This reaching for metaphor is characteristic of Larkin when, at a turning point of a poem, he is attempting to bring a general sense of things into focus. It is equally characteristic that he later rejects the metaphor, preferring to stay with realistic detail or just plain statement. Immediately below this passage he wrote a prose note to himself:

Where do those innate ideas come
from, that take half a lifetime to
realise, by which time it's too
late to do anything about them?

The first clause of this piece of prose, with "assumptions" in place of "ideas", was to take its place in the completed poem. In the meantime, after some heavy drafting, the words became associated with yet another figurative attempt, "Where do these/Innate compulsions, like a spine or grain/Derive?" On the way, Larkin had tried out another comparison that underwent a good deal of correction but did not stay: "They cradle us as feathers do the bird/That grows them".

During these very extensive draftings of what became the beginning of his penultimate stanza, Larkin had also tried out a picture of the older Dockery as self-satisfied bourgeois — a further misdirection: "He will stand/Swagged with directorships, obese/With oil-fired". This attempt (which possibly reveals that Larkin felt oil-fired central heating was a desirable luxury in those days) was not carried to completion. In all, Larkin started out on this stanza seven times before getting to the end of it and moving on to his conclusion; and, even after that, he made further corrections to it.

One phrase that came early and stayed was "To me it was (meant) dilution". The conception of marriage and an heir as dilution is an unusual one. It seems to imply, in "Dockery and Son", a dilution of identity. The metaphor is encountered, in association with similar contemplations, in a book that Larkin must certainly have known in his youth, Virginia Woolf's *To the Lighthouse*. Lily Briscoe, the artist who did not marry, reflects: "she need not marry . . . she need not undergo that degradation. She was saved from that dilution."[3]

The bulk of the draftings of this fifth stanza so far examined took place on February 19th. On 27th February and 1st March, Larkin continued through three pages to work on the same stanza and his first attempts to move on from it. The density of effort can be seen in the following passage:

```
                        Not from what
            think truest    most desire want
       We most believe or what we want to do:
                                    merely a style  more a
            that hopelessly  It's only added where  style
      Those They twist out of shape.  Whatever rouses
                        Through which to express life
 We knit our lives to  We have to use or don't live, at all
          Us beside the breaking sea of clouds of and houses  all the
      Feeling    limit \We must express life in, though/    while
      Knowing it drag us. . . . Or rather, not
                  /  falsify
```

those   They're
They twist ~~that~~ hopelessly. / ~~It's~~ more a style
      by ~~through~~
We have to live ~~within~~, / knowing all the while
   useless   remote
How ~~false~~ and ~~limiting~~ . . . Or rather, not

            unforeseeable
All the while / just ~~now and then~~   days
      midway
That tail / off ~~half~~

Having reached a phrase that was to have an important place in the
final argument of the poem, "They're more a style/Our lives adopt",
he attempted a new direction—the evocation of scenes in which a
person comes to realise the direction his life has taken:

      mornings, perhaps, or evenings;
           ~~meek~~ smudged
The sky great ruined districts; the ~~docile~~ / town
    you   dreamed   — ~~sweet~~ shops
Somewhere ~~one~~ never ~~thought~~ of ~~going~~ ~~cigarettes~~,   lodgings;
          what
~~And~~ Just to be there sums up ~~all~~ you've done.

The writing has the authentic Larkin sadness; but, after returning
to the poem on March 1st and making two more attempts in this
direction, he stopped work on the poem with the lines

Free, or not happy, or committed to
   A   some
~~Some~~ district of a dark unsought town.

The next day he started drafting the last stanza of "Long Last",
a poem begun before "Dockery and Son". He continued with "Long
Last" two days later; but, in the middle of the page, he drew a line
and went back to "Dockery and Son".

Convinced he was he should be added to!
Why did he think adding meant increase?
To me it was dilution. Where do these
Innate assumptions come from? Not from what
We think truest or most want to do:
Those fracture helplessly
~~They twist those hopelessly~~. They're more a style
Our lives bring with them; hidden for a while/,

> ~~Are seen through gaps opening   between~~
> ~~They come to light in retrospect,   as, not~~
> ~~They come to light as curves to what we're for~~
>   ~~infancy~~
> ~~By growing growing   They're suddenly around us~~
> ~~They rear like sandclouds~~
> ~~They suddenly surround us~~
> Suddenly they harden into ~~what~~ we've got
>   all

The metaphor of the "curves" re-emerges, to be rejected again; but the image of the "sand clouds", which will be adopted, finally appears. Larkin stops at a crucial phrase: "harden into all we've got". Returning to the poem the next day, Larkin is tempted by another figurative comparison, "Away from what we hoped for, like air trails". However, the following day the conclusion finally begins to emerge:

>   got
> And how we ~~get~~ it; and when we turn they rear
>   blocking   ~~retreat~~
> Like sandclouds, ~~shutting~~ the way back, ~~in the~~ bodying
> For Dockery a son, for me nothing.
>   ~~rigid rails weave~~   The rails weave out of sight A   called
> ~~The lines weave out of sight   -?   -?~~   ~~My~~ train is ~~due~~
> In life, after boredom comes fear.
> ~~The steps~~ break off we ~~came climbed break off What brings us here,~~
> Whatever brought us there and something else,   ~~breaks off~~
> Whether or not we meant the past, its gone,
>   ~~And~~ What's left of time
> ~~What's left will be the same over again.~~

Here Larkin attempts to link the conclusion with the scene on the railway station by making explicit the metaphorical force of the railway lines — another figurative attempt that was not retained.

Ten days later, on March 15th, Larkin brings the drafting to a conclusion, dating it "16.3.63". The penultimate stanza is as printed, except that "hidden" was to be replaced by "habit" and "warp tight-shut, like doors" has not yet arrived. In its place is the phrase "crumble helplessly", modified from "fracture helplessly". Rather oddly, this unusual phrase occurred in a popular song that nobody could help hearing in the radio-dominated days of the nineteen-forties — in the Ink Spots' "Bless You for Being an Angel". It is just possible that it resided in Larkin's memory to re-emerge here. The conclusion is not as we know it:

And how we got it; ~~and~~ when we turn, they rear
                              blocking
Like sandclouds, ~~block blurring~~ the way back, bodying
For Dockery a son, for me nothing,
            with
Nothing ~~has~~ all a son's harsh here-and-now.
~~Life matures from boredom into fear~~ Life is first boredom,/ then
~~In life, after boredom comes fear~~ then ~~after that~~   fear.
                                   ~~after that~~

            ~~life time is~~ ~~life~~ we use ~~time~~ it
Whether ~~we used~~ ~~time~~ or not / it goes,
~~And twists~~
~~Making~~   ~~makes of~~ us to
Twisting~~And sees that we~~   the element we chose,
            And we are dead before we quite see how.

This was not the end of work on the poem. After making a further draft of the last stanza of "Long Last" on March 18th, Larkin made a new attempt at the opening of the fourth stanza of "Dockery and Son":

Unhindered moon. To have no son, no wife
No house or land still seemed quite natural,
~~through~~ a   echoed with
Only ~~The~~ numbness ~~could I have~~ the shock
Of finding out how far I'd gone with life

He then returned to his conclusion:

And how we got it; looked back on they rear
                              close
            ~~startlingly~~ and ~~-?- en~~
Like sandclouds ~~towering~~   ~~up~~   embodying
                  thick   ~~startlingly~~
For Dockery a son, for me nothing,
                              patronage
~~But~~ Nothing with all a son's harsh here-and-now
Life is first boredom, then fear.
Whether or not we use it, it goes,
      in   leaves us
~~And at the end we're left with what we chose~~
~~Or what it chose for us~~

And makes   had   known
Making us what we ~~did~~ not ~~know~~ we chose,
And ending us before we quite see how.

110 LARKIN AT WORK

What it leaves us
~~What~~
And ~~And~~ we ~~become~~ is never what we chose
But what chose us, like an inheritance, like age.

It must have been when Larkin decided to end his last line with "age" that he went back and changed a "son's harsh here-and-now" to the mysterious but effective "son's harsh patronage". Finally, on March 28th, he rewrote the aphoristic conclusion, of which he was so proud:[4]

Nothing, with all a son's harsh patronage.
Life is first boredom, then fear,
Whether or not we use it, it goes,
⟨we⟩without knowing it
Leav~~ingAnd leaves~~ what we ~~peculiarly~~ chose
only
And age, and then the ~~bitter~~ end of age.

The change from "bitter" to the more muted "only" makes the line even sadder. The redrafting from "we peculiarly chose" to "we without knowing it chose" makes it clear that the version of this phrase in the printed poem, "something hidden from us chose", was not meant to imply that we are ruled by forces beyond ourselves, but was probably introduced to get rid of the awkward rhythm and articulation of the phrase "we without", with its two words beginning in "w".

There is no "fair" version of the last part of the poem; and the conclusion was evidently revised in typescript. The poem is a triumph in the realistic meditative narrative form that admirers came to find typical of Larkin. Its drafting exemplifies a pattern often encountered in Larkin's work on his longer poems. After the rapid and felicitous writing of the first four of his six stanzas, Larkin is caught up in attempt after attempt at his penultimate stanza — the stanza in which the meaning of the experience that began the poem is revealed. When he has made that resolution, he drafts his concluding stanza with much less trouble.

A couple of months later, Larkin started to write "The Dance", a poem about going to a ball, evidently the University of Hull Staff Sports Club Dance of May 10th, 1963, attended by a woman to whom he was attracted. The poem was never completed. After forty pages and nearly a year of drafting, Larkin made a typescript of the twelve stanzas that he had completed, and it was evidently from this that the version in *Collected Poems* was prepared. Another eight near complete lines, not in the typescript, come at the end of his drafting:

How the flash palaces fill up like caves
With tidal hush of dresses, and the sharp
And secretive excitement running through
          ritual
Their open ~~ang~~ that can alter to
Anguish so easily against the carp
Of too-explicit music, till
I see for the first time as something whole
What earlier seemed safely divisible

There are many arresting passages, even among those rejected from Larkin's typescript:

          genial intercourse
By a symbolic interchange of wives
(Provided they get sitters), can act young —
But is it acting that creates a sense
Of something snapped off short, that arches tense
And aching from the gullet to the tongue?

The stanza form is complex, as in "The Whitsun Weddings"; but this does not seem to be the cause of Larkin's difficulties. He appears to be preoccupied with too many impulses and to be unable to bring them to a coherence.

The poem, like "Dockery and Son", is in the "novelistic" manner typical of many successes of Larkin's middle period, where the articulation of psychological and sociological perception and the bringing alive of perceived detail are so important. The last drafting is on a page dated "12.5.64". It concludes Workbook No. 6. The next poem was begun on October 6th in Workbook No. 7. It came to be "Solar".

While the composition of the poem is not particularly interesting, its first page is symptomatic of a change:

⊢ ⊬	
~~Lion face spilling~~	∪ − ∪ − ∪ −
~~From~~	∪ − ∪ − ∪ −
~~Spilling lion face~~	∪ − ∪ − ∪ −
	− ∪ ∪ ∪ − ∪
Suspended lion face	∪ ∪ ∪ − ∪ ∪
~~That spills~~ at	∪ − ∪ − ∪ −
Spilling ~~Spilling from~~ the centre	∪ − ∪ −
an	∪ − ∪ − ∪
Of ~~long~~ unfurnished sky	− ∪ − ∪ −
~~Your limitless regard~~	

~~Your own intense regard~~
     Explosion of
~~Your exploding~~ regard
     How still you stand,
~~You are stationary~~

And how unaided,
     single stalkless
~~A thread~~ of   ~~jar~~ flower
~~Pouring~~   ~~burning bag~~
     Rough head of flames
~~Pouring incessantly~~
Pouring   unrecognised
~~And how~~ ~~unrecompensed~~
   Into
~~Over~~ deep scoops of sea
    On   of
~~The~~ shrug~~ged up~~ mountains
      ~~forests~~ ~~letting fall~~   The cities
~~The lands, the eyes~~ ~~Forestfuls of eyes~~. full of eyes.

The next day he wrote out his first seven lines without correction:

Suspended lionface,
Spilling at the centre
Of an unfurnished sky;
How still you stand,
And how unaided,
Single stalkless flower,
~~Rough hands of flame~~

The first six lines are as in the printed version. The heavy drafting
of the opening page had alongside it, as shown, a metrical pattern.
The exact relationship of this to what was completed is not clear;
but it attests to the fact that the incantatory effect of this poem
was a dominant guide in the drafting. In this respect, whatever one
may think of the poem, we see a radically new departure in idiom
for Larkin, in contrast with the realist idiom of "Dockery and Son"
and "The Dance" and so much that had gone before them, where the
effect of the poems depends on a simulation of the shifts of tone and
rhythm of the natural speaking voice of an often dramatised speaker.

One is tempted to say that Larkin must have become in some way
dissatisfied with his old idiom; but that is hardly supported by the way
in which he comes back to it in many of his best later poems, including
"To the Sea", "Show Saturday" and the final "Aubade". However,

another slightly later poem that shows Larkin trying a decidedly new manner was "The Explosion". Introducing his reading of it in 1972, Larkin said: "What I should like to do is write different kinds of poem that might be by different people . . . That's why I've chosen to read now a poem that isn't especially "like" me, or like what I fancy I'm supposed to be like".[5]

The Explosion

On the day of the explosion
Shadows pointed towards the pithead:
In the sun the slagheap slept.

Down the lane came men in pitboots
Coughing oath-edged talk and pipe-smoke,
Shouldering off the freshened silence.

One chased after rabbits; lost them;
Came back with a nest of lark's eggs;
Showed them; lodged them in the grasses.

So they passed in beards and moleskins,
Fathers, brothers, nicknames, laughter,
Through the tall gates standing open.

At noon, there came a tremor; cows
Stopped chewing for a second; sun,
Scarfed as in a heat-haze, dimmed.

The dead go on before us, they
Are sitting in God's house in comfort,
We shall see them face to face —

Plain as lettering in the chapels
It was said, and for a second
Wives saw men of the explosion

Larger than in life they managed —
Gold as on a coin, or walking
Somehow from the sun towards them,

One showing the eggs unbroken.

The poem indeed differed from the type of poem that people had come to expect of Larkin, in that it worked importantly by the interacting of images and did not conclude, as "Church Going" and "Dockery and Son" had done, with a summary conclusion, but instead presented an image encountered earlier in the poem. It also involved

the use of an unusual metre, the trochaic tetrameter of Longfellow's
The Song of Hiawatha.

That metre is not in evidence in the earliest drafting, though some
of the details that were to be part of the final poem are there:

> The dew was shaken ~~off~~ the hedge
> By the ~~explosion~~
>
> ?
>
>   on
> In the morning ~~of~~ the day of the explosion
> The shadows were long, and pointed towards the pithead
>   out
> The men were striding ~~for~~ in their great boots
> Sending a lark up almost vertically
> The notes ~~in~~ coming down like ~~dew~~ shaken dew
>
>   from
> One of them chased a rabbit ~~at~~ the side of the road,
> Kicking up spray, but it eluded him
> As the men laughed their teeth were white
> They left the smell of pipesmoke on the air

The metre begins to emerge in the second attempt at the opening:

> On the day of the explosion
> Shadows pointed towards the pithead:
>   ~~singing shook~~
> ~~A lark rose / in circles down singing~~
>   ~~Slagheaps were bald in the sun~~
> Striding In the sun bald slagheaps slept
>   / Groups of ~~striding~~ men in ~~boots~~ pitboots
> Threw ~~off~~ behind them speech and
>   ~~Kicked up spray, left behind~~ smoking
>   strong   the gentle
> ~~And~~ At / odds ~~strongly~~ with ~~the~~ / morning.
>
>   ~~Threw off —————— of speech and smoking~~

The drafting here begins to be aimed at attaining the trochaic metre,
as in the line that Larkin corrects to become "Striding groups of men
in pitboots".

The above first page of drafting is dated "7.12.69". On Christmas
Day, Larkin returned to the poem. His first three lines were now as
they are in the printed version, except that "slagheaps" was plural.
The three-line stanza is established as the pattern of the poem:

On the day of the explosion
Shadows pointed towards the pithead:
In the sun the slagheaps slept.

      the
      Down lanes
~~Down~~ Up lanes,   came ~~dow~~
    ~~Striding groups of~~ men in pit boots
Coughing ~~Throwing off~~ ~~pungent~~ sharpened pipesmoke
Scattering ~~Threw behind them~~ / speech and ~~smoking~~
    .Jostling   ~~the fresh~~
    ~~Both at odds with~~ ~~the fresh~~ silence:
          ~~morning~~
          the fresh

      for a
    ~~chased a rabbit——~~
      ~~up~~
    went ~~after~~ rabbits,   kicking ~~up spray~~
    One ~~kicked up spray, chasing a rabbits,~~
spray:
    Another found a nest ~~showing~~
  He ~~showed~~ the whole eggs
    ~~The eggs unbroken~~ in his hand.
~~Showing~~ He showed

    So   ~~nick~~names
~~Then~~ they passed, their ~~knives~~ and moleskins   sons
    hand   beards and laughter,
Knives ~~and~~ kerchiefs, ~~teeth and beards,~~   nicknames
    a Through the iron set-open gates
~~And the lark came down in circles.~~

          cows
At noon there was a tremor: ~~sheep~~
  Stopped eating
~~Looked up~~   for a second: sun,
    as
Scarfed / in a heat-haze, dimmed.   the hooter

Evening shadows pointed backwards
  ~~The~~ Black shawled women, leading children,
~~All afternoon~~
  Went up
~~We trod the~~ lanes the men had come down

Like a ~~small~~ country fair dispersing
But so slow, with such white faces.

Names began to be ~~important~~ repeated
~~And real names~~

Real names now, in ⟋ newsprint;
⟋ ~~?~~ ~~type~~
Copperplate in Bibles, sealed in
    sanded letters,
~~In letters~~ ⟋ ~~?~~

The metre is set; and some of the changes are made to sustain it, as with the rather awkward "Through the iron set-open gates". As Larkin gets the feel of the metre, the lines come in a form that he feels less need to change. The stanza in which the tremor occurs is as in the final version, except for "eating" instead of "chewing". Unusual for Larkin are the notes to himself— "sons", "nicknames", "the hooter" — alongside lines into which they might be fitted. Most importantly, perhaps, he has found the image of the nest of lark's eggs, which is to be so important structurally in the poem.

Larkin drew a line, and then continued, presumably on the same day:

Next Sunday in the chapels preachers
                are
Cried: The dead ~~were~~ yet immortal:
    shall meet
We ~~should see~~ them face to face,

            women
And some ~~widows~~ kept this vision;
Half a century later, still

                held that saying
And some widows ~~kept this vision~~
All their lives (some left the district,
                /died
Went to pieces, ~~drank~~, remarried),

    Saw
~~Seeing~~ the men of the explosion
Gold as on a coin, or walking
Somehow in the sun towards them,

        showing
(One ~~holding~~ the eggs unbroken),
~~Bringing~~
~~Running down the pointed shadows.~~

The words describing the dead are beginning to emerge; though their attribution to the preacher will be dropped. The suggestion that the wives will later repeat them will also be dropped, along with the reference to their future. Much that is most felicitous in the poem comes with little need for correction. The last three lines of the poem are there in final form, with the last line, which brings back the image of the lark's eggs, standing alone, as it does in the printed version.

On Boxing Day, Larkin started on a new page to write out a fair version of the poem, completing it on the next page, which is dated at its head "5.1.70".

On the day of the explosion
Shadows pointed towards the pithead:
In the sun the slagheaps slept.

Down the lane came men in pitboots
          oath
Coughing ~~sharp~~-edged talk and pipesmoke,
Shouldering off   ened
~~Jostling~~ the fresh / silence.

       after rabbits   them
One chased ~~a young rabbit~~; lost ~~him~~;
Came back with a nest of lark's eggs;
Showed it   in ~~in by~~ grasses   ~~ditch~~ hedge
~~Set~~ it ~~softly on~~ the ~~ground grass on~~.
lodged

       their names
       ~~jackknives~~
So they passed, ~~nicknames~~ and moleskins,
~~Husbands,~~   ~~jackknives~~ nicknames
Fathers ~~Sons and knifeblades, beards and~~ laughter
     the   brothers
Through / ~~the iron~~ gates set ~~wide~~ open.
lettered

       a
At noon there came ~~the~~ tremor, cows
Stopped chewing for a second; sun,
Scarfed as in a heat-haze, dimmed.

Evening shadows pointed backwards.
Blackshawled women, leading children,
Climbed the lane men had come down/

Like a country fair dispersing/
(But so slow, and such white faces,),
~~Going~~ Back to ~~silent~~ houses stopped like clocks.

The dead have gone before us, they
    Are waiting in God's house in comfort
~~Are sit waiting in the next valley;~~
We shall see them face to face —

Plain as lettering in the chapels
It was said, and listening women
Saw the men of the explosion

Gold as on a coin, or walking
Somehow in the sun towards them
(One showing the eggs unbroken).

This is the final version in the Workbook. There is no concluding date to indicate that the poem is finished. The first six stanzas are as in the printed version, or close to it; though the "lettered gates" were to be replaced by the more evocative "tall gates". Larkin had retained the two stanzas about the women coming to the pithead, which he may reluctantly have eliminated later to tighten the poem: the rejected "Back to silent houses stopped like clocks" is one of the most moving phrases in the whole drafting. Oddly, Larkin had changed his very effective ending, where the last line, which so potently brings back the image of the "lark's eggs", had stood alone. He was to return to this effect in the printed version. Some redrafting and compression were evidently made when the poem was transferred to the typewriter. There exists a typescript, which is the same as the printed version, except that the italicised passage is not italicised, and it has "Plainer than life", which was changed to "Larger than life", presumably to avoid the repetition of "Plain" in two adjacent stanzas.

    This very moving poem, the entire drafting of which is given here, came surprisingly rapidly, once Larkin had found his metre, just as did parts of "Dockery and Son". However, the contrast between these two poems shows the extent to which Larkin had moved, in some of his later poems, into a new idiom.

Chapter 9

POEMS OF AGING

Four poems concerned with old age, sickness and death constitute Larkin's last major block of composition. "How" was begun and completed on April 10th 1970. It was followed by "The Building", begun on December 14th 1971 and completed February 9th 1972. "Heads in the Women's Ward" was begun and completed on March 6th 1972; and "The Old Fools" was begun on September 12th 1972 and completed on January 12th 1973. The periods separating some of the poems may seem long, but they come in close proximity in the Workbooks. Each of the longer poems was preceded by the shorter poem on a similar theme that Larkin did not choose to collect, presumably because he felt that the shorter poems were in some way overshadowed or superseded by the longer ones.

How

How high they build hospitals!
Lighted cliffs, against dawns
Of days people will die on.
I can see one from here.

How cold winter keeps
And long, ignoring
Our need now for kindness.
Spring has got into the wrong year.

How few people are,
Held apart by acres
Of housing, and children
With their shallow violent eyes.

"How" contains the phrase "Lighted cliffs", giving an image taken up in "The Building"; and indeed the whole drift of its first two stanzas is absorbed into the later poem, whose first word "Higher" echoes the opening of "How".

How high they build hospitals
I can see one from here
A lighted cliff

The entire drafting of "How" and "Heads in the Women's Ward" is given, but not that of the other poems discussed in this chapter.

How high they build hospitals!
           in front of
Lighted cliffs ~~against~~ grape-dark skies
On shallow morning shores, littered with clouds.

How high they build hospitals!
Lighted cliffs steady/against the pale
        ~~mornings~~
Cloud-littered ~~shores of ships~~ early skies
on mornings
    /When someone is always dying

How high they build hospitals!
          against
Lighted cliffs ~~on~~ mornings
    ~~someone is~~ there's always somebody
    ~~there's~~
When ~~some always someone~~ dying.
I can see one from here.

     long   are
How ~~cold the~~ winters ~~stays~~
And how cold, ignoring
That you can't stand it for ever.
Spring is late, like a train.

                  are
How few people there ~~will be~~
      ~~far apart~~
And how ~~far apart~~ separated
~~By~~   ~~How many~~
~~Among~~ ~~Among~~   housing estates of children
  By With their shallow violent eyes!

"How high" and "Lighted cliffs", the phrases that were to be echoed in "The Building", came immediately in their final form in the drafting of "How", and were the starting point for the poem.

"How" is one of the few poems for which there exists a typescript on which Larkin did fairly extensive correction in handwriting:

How high they build hospitals!
Lighted cliffs against dawns
Of days people will die on.
I see one from here.

How cold winters keep
And long, ignoring

                    of kind climates
          Our need ~~to be quiet now.~~
          Spring is held back, somewhere.

          How few people are,
Separated
     ~~Parted~~ by   ~~Held apart by~~ acres
                    ~~And widely separated~~
                              and
          Of ~~By~~ housing estates, ~~of~~ children
          With violent shallow eyes.

As can be seen, the version that might be reconstructed from this differs both from the version that might be reconstructed from the Workbook drafting and from the final printed version. This is unusual, in that most of Larkin's surviving typescripts are close to or identical with the printed version and have few annotations.

The entire drafting of the poem was done on one page of the Workbook and presumably in one go; followed by the work on the typescript. Further work evidently occurred in making a final typescript for publication. Nonetheless, this contrasts with the work on "The Building", which takes up the same material, but was written over a period of nearly two months and which occupies seventeen pages in Workbooks No. 7 and No. 8.

The Building

          Higher than the handsomest hotel
          The lucent comb shows up for miles, but see,
          All round it close-ribbed streets rise and fall
          Like a great sigh out of the last century.
          The porters are scruffy; what keep drawing up
          At the entrance are not taxis; and in the hall
          As well as creepers hangs a frightening smell.

          There are paperbacks, and tea at so much a cup,
          Like an airport lounge, but those who tamely sit
          On rows of steel chairs turning the ripped mags
          Haven't come far. More like a local bus,
          These outdoor clothes and half-filled shopping bags
          And faces restless and resigned, although
          Every few minutes comes a kind of nurse

          To fetch someone away: the rest refit
          Cups back to saucers, cough, or glance below
          Seats for dropped gloves or cards. Humans, caught
          On ground curiously neutral, homes and names

Suddenly in abeyance; some are young,
Some old, but most at that vague age that claims
The end of choice, the last of hope; and all

Here to confess that something has gone wrong.
It must be error of a serious sort,
For see how many floors it needs, how tall
It's grown by now, and how much money goes
In trying to correct it. See the time,
Half-past eleven on a working day,
And these picked out of it; see, as they climb

To their appointed levels, how their eyes
Go to each other, guessing; on the way
Someone's wheeled past, in washed-to-rags ward clothes:
They see him, too. They're quiet. To realise
This new thing held in common makes them quiet,
For past these doors are rooms, and rooms past those,
And more rooms yet, each one further off

And harder to return from; and who knows
Which he will see, and when? For the moment, wait,
Look down at the yard. Outside seems old enough:
Red brick, lagged pipes, and someone walking by it
Out to the car park, free. Then, past the gate,
Traffic; a locked church; short terraced streets
Where kids chalk games, and girls with hair-dos fetch

Their separates from the cleaners — O world,
Your loves, your chances, are beyond the stretch
Of any hand from here! And so, unreal,
A touching dream to which we all are lulled
But wake from separately. In it, conceits
And self-protecting ignorance congeal
To carry life, collapsing only when

Called to these corridors (for now once more
The nurse beckons —). Each gets up and goes
At last. Some will be out by lunch, or four;
Others, not knowing it, have come to join
The unseen congregations whose white rows
Lie set apart above — women, men;
Old, young; crude facets of the only coin

This place accepts. All know they are going to die.
Not yet, perhaps not here, but in the end,
And somewhere like this. That is what it means,
This clean-sliced cliff; a struggle to transcend
The thought of dying, for unless its powers

Outbuild cathedrals nothing contravenes
The coming dark, though crowds each evening try

With wasteful, weak, propitiatory flowers.

The first lines of the drafting of "The Building", begun on December 14th 1971, contain not only Larkin's first line, but many of the details that were to take their place in the first and second stanzas of the final version of the poem.

Higher than the handsomest hotel: yet
                                    keep
The porters are scruffy, and what ~~are~~ drawing up
Under the portico are not taxis.
                        more like an airport
Cross the hall to the desk: is it / ~~an airstation~~?
                                in rows
~~A paperback stand; people are sitting about~~
~~But the air has a frightening smell,~~
~~And the people could never afford the fare.~~

After a second attempt, Larkin wrote out this first stanza without alteration and then proceeded to draft a second stanza.

        do
Nor ~~are~~   look
~~And~~ the people who sit in rows ~~are not~~ rich
                near
In the hall, upstairs ~~at~~ Enquiries, and then
                        have to
Repeatedly round corners they ~~sit wait~~ wait on chairs
    In outdoor clothes, as if ~~a bus has stopped~~ in a stopped bus
~~As is in a stopped bus, in outdoor clothes.~~
                    the old
    Housewives, ~~old people,~~
~~Some have cups of tea,~~ a schoolgirl, working men,
All with something in common (which

Is something wrong), all with the same belief
That here will cure them. Tea is available. As
They drink, someone is wheeled by, gowned
And clutching a bloody bowl

Once again, some of the details, such as "outdoor clothes" and the comparison to sitting in a "bus", were to stay with the poem. The link into the beginning of a third stanza with "All with something in common (which//Is something wrong)" — is a first shot at "all/Here to confess that something has gone wrong", which begins the *fourth* stanza of the final version. Larkin stopped drafting with the image "someone is wheeled by, gowned/And clutching a bloody bowl" — material that in fact took its place in a modified form in the *fifth* stanza.

It may well be that Larkin felt that the poem was developing too rapidly or too sketchily. Up to then, he had not finalised his rhyme scheme. It was at this point that he seems to have arrived at the notion of a scheme that linked his stanzas by having a rhyme scheme complete itself in eight lines while the stanzas completed themselves in seven lines. This necessitated a poem that would last for eight stanzas, if the rhyme scheme was to conclude at the last line of the final stanza. He may have then seen the consequent need to pace his material, so as to fit it to the length required by the highly constricting rhyme scheme. He drew a line and redrafted the first stanza:

> Higher than the handsomest hotel,
> The ~~tall~~   lucent comb ~~standing~~ shows up
> ~~It shines for miles~~ ~~is seen~~ for miles; but see
> The close-   all round it
> /Ribbed streets ~~in close formation~~ rise and fall
> Like a great sigh out of the last century;
> ~~And~~ The porters are scruffy, and what keep drawing up
> At the entrance are not taxis, and in the hall
> As well as palms there is a frightening smell.

The pictorial elements are more developed. The "lucent comb" recalls the "lighted cliff" of "How"; while the "Ribbed streets . . . rise and fall/Like a great sigh out of the last century" came from earlier draftings in the workbooks. They had emerged before three times: once in January 1962, in the midst of the drafting of an uncompleted poem, "Under a Cloud"; once on 17th October 1967, in another uncompleted poem, "Driving North through Autumn"; and yet again in an uncollected poem, "Clouds, Dwelling Places, Light", from early in 1971. Larkin must have been rather proud of these lines, as such Eliotian reuse of rejected scraps was unusual for him.

On Christmas Eve, Larkin returned to the poem and his second stanza:

> There are paperbacks/ and tea at so much a cup/,
>   an air terminal
> Like ~~a departure lounge~~, but those who sit
> On rows of steel ~~framed~~ chairs turning the ripped mags
>   come ~~come~~ far /It's more like a stopped bus

Haven't ~~left home on holiday~~ It's ~~more like~~ A ~~stopped bus~~
~~Are not travellers.~~   travellers perhaps
~~Would have their~~ The With and ~~the and~~ half-filled
might~~The~~ / outdoor clothes, ~~the half-filled~~ shopping bags,
        faces   and yet
And ~~eyes~~, restless and resigned, ~~but not~~
    Every few minutes comes a sort of nurse
~~The linking sense of something wrong with us~~

    To
~~And~~ calls someone away.

The changes do not appear consequential and in no way affect the direction of the poem: it is a matter of getting the right phrases for the details that evoke the setting. None of these phrases functions metaphorically in the poem, except in so far as they contribute to the suggestive power of "the building". That sinister suggestiveness emerges in the turning phrase "To call someone away".

Larkin then made a fair version of the stanza and drafted his next stanza with little correction. The only part showing much work is the passage that became one of the most evocative in the poem: "that vague age that claims/The last of choice, the last of hope".

Returning to the poem on December 28th, Larkin gave the poem its title, "The Building", and made a fair version of his drafting to date. With the phrase, "Here to confess that something has gone wrong", Larkin enters difficult territory.

Here to confess that something has gone wrong.
                    and   while 'phones report
Lights flash; lifts climb ~~or~~ sink; ~~someone is brought~~.
    There are many floors, and passages
~~Past holding a bloody bowl~~

Here to confess that something has gone wrong.
This is ~~This human~~   of a
    A ~~Humans in~~   error ~~of a~~ serious sort.
        ~~Take note~~
For see~~For see~~ how many floors there are, how tall
                    is
The building ~~stands~~, and how much money goes
                        ~~Past~~   once inside
                    ~~Behind~~ ~~these doors~~   ~~you are here~~
    In trying to correct it. ~~Enter in~~ ~~Once~~
        ~~will~~ starts half-shies with
            starts
The body ~~knows~~ shying ~~like~~ a horse's ~~in~~ dread

                                                    ~~being~~
           ~~such importance each door~~   ~~it senses guesses~~ / ~~its~~
      At ~~Of what's behind the doors,~~   ~~what surrounds it being~~ ~~identified~~
           guessing it's to be identified

                         ~~man in a dressing gown~~
           ~~Against its will with a man with a bloody bowl~~
                         ~~bloody bowl~~
           ~~Wheeled past with a lolling head~~ and lolling head
              ~~The steam, the beds in the white receding rows,~~
           ~~The woman who keeps wandering off, and those~~
             white ~~the wandering~~ woman wandering ~~receding~~ up and down
                   ~~all ?~~
           ~~In /~~ ~~unreal rows~~ ~~glimpsed in white serried rows~~
                         ~~smiling~~

The orientation implied by "confess" will be important to the tone of
the poem, suggesting as it does that those who come to "the building" want to hide something that it is the activity of "the building"
to reveal. The word also has religious associations that come into
play here. Larkin then made a fair version from the above drafting,
replacing "human error of a serious sort" with "error of a serious
sort", with its hidden suggestion of original sin. The reaction at seeing oneself mirrored in those already there— "The body half-shies
with a horse's dread" —leads on to further disturbing details of the
place, the first of them revived from the opening draft of the poem:
a "man in a dressing gown/Wheeled past with a bloody bowl and
lolling head./The stick held stiffened old, munching, and those/Who
stare about and wander up and down". A bird that comes to "peck/A
moment, gulping, then fly off" introduces a comparison with the outside world "that is real as long as nothing breaks"; though, when we
"lurch/On to the wrong rail", "This tower is all that matters". The
figurative use of the shying horse and the wrong rail were both to go
before the final version. Larkin was again drawn to figurative expressions to evoke key feelings, but, as almost always, dropped them to let
his poems work through the realistic details of his scenes. The contrast with the outside world, with its "abandoned" (later "locked")
"churches" was the way forward for the poem; but, to judge from the
intensity of the drafting and deletions, Larkin was not sure of this.

                                   Out there
           Is real only as long as nothing breaks
                    cooperating; once the lurch
           Or stops ~~or starts to separate~~

~~once off the~~ away from
Onto the wrong rail comes, ~~away from~~ straight,
~~Once~~ Then
This tower is all that matters. ~~Then~~ there wakes
A A
~~The~~ The small and growing visionary seed
wherein ~~our~~ death sits tiny credible
~~Of whirling to destruction~~ and ~~visible,~~

And / not
~~And~~ bigger than the world: ~~Not~~ others' death,   briefness of all
From which comes change and requiem, but dull   ~~lent~~
dark ~~This~~ Therefore this clean-sliced   ~~brief held~~
And lasting ~~end.It will happen.So this~~ cliff ~~and half believing~~
~~lit~~ twinkling with terror,   ~~belief~~ of
~~Clean sliced and lit with terror~~   ~~and faith~~
~~at dawn and dusk~~   faltering
~~brief held~~   and ~~?~~   breath
failing
the dark irrelevant weed
Is born above ~~the abandoned churches, and~~
~~outsoars~~
~~Stare over the irrelevant city~~
~~streets housing~~
~~The~~ Of ~~habitation~~   and abandoned churches

After this extensive redrafting on January 5th and an attempt at a mere five lines on January 9th, the poem was given up temporarily. Larkin may have felt stuck; though the work taken up on January 10th was "Going, Going", which Larkin had promised for a report entitled "How Do We Want to Live", which was presented to the Secretary of State for the Environment in January 1972. Larkin evidently came to regret this, as he found it interfering with his work on "The Building".[1]

On January 13th, Larkin resumed work on "The Building" with a strategy that he often employed when the way forward seemed difficult: he made a fair version of everything he had done so far — six-and-a-half stanzas in all. He also gave the poem a new title, "The Meeting House", not presumably with the intention of evoking Quaker overtones, but with the idea of capturing the feeling that the building is the place where we all come together to face our ultimate fate. On the page on which this drafting concluded, he wrote: "We must never die. No one must ever die." — a rather violently categorical statement that embodied a feeling potent for him: it was taken up later, and was in key with the very tense expressions of the apprehension of death that Larkin had developed, but which did not find a place in the completed poem. Indeed, the published poem comes round to a resigned contradiction of Larkin's note, with its simple "All know they are going to die".

After crossing out his fourth stanza and making some corrections to the rest, Larkin recommenced work on the poem on January 15th, beginning with his fourth stanza. He now numbered the stanzas; perhaps as an aid in making his poem fit the required length; but it may also be a sign of confidence in what he had done. The shying horse has gone, to be replaced by the mundane detail "Half-past eleven on a working day"; and all that is left of the images of the other patients is

> washed-to-rags
> Someone's wheeled past, in ~~faded, washed~~ ward clothes

Stanza 6, with its contrasting images of the world outside is quickly reached in near final form. However, the transition in stanza 7 leads at this point to further reflection on the finality of death:

> Their separates from the cleaners — O world
> Your love, your chances, are beyond the stretch
> Of any hand from here! And you are all.
> Nothing is left once this life is annulled,
> Except the certainty that what now meets
>   Do
> In us then parts for ever. ~~Do~~ we recall
> That
> ~~This~~ truth about each other only when
> The

>   see
>   ~~now~~
> Within   But ~~turn~~ once
> ~~Bought to~~ this clean-sliced cliff? ~~Turn back~~ / more:
>   Each one goes alone
> The nurse ~~is~~ beckoning. ~~We all go in turn~~
>   will
> Some ~~to~~ be out by lunch; some here till four;
>   and longer ~~to join~~ ~~joining~~ the strange
>   ~~to join that congregation~~
> Some for the night: ~~all come back in the end~~
>   \joining/
> ~~Dispersed~~ Congregation dispersed

>   ~~No one must ever die.~~

The poem was again set aside for the completion of "Going, Going". He returned to "The Building" on January 29th to draft the penultimate and final stanzas. The latter evidently took some getting into:

there ~~first~~   can
From ~~Here~~ / they ~~will first~~
~~a~~ broken down. ~~in~~   ~~And from it is~~   descry
When ~~the ? brings them here.~~   ~~they meet~~
distant
Loss like a ~~far~~ reef
~~The loss to come;~~ / loss, first, of things
deep
Then loss of self the / vague frost of death
~~Then loss of self;~~   ~~both drawing closer~~
~~That melts~~ hope to nothing   ~~then settles~~ on faces, that
~~Settling on faces~~   settling   ~~into nothing~~ ~~and~~ on melting brings
~~An endlessly —~~ ~~Diverging~~ absence   Their loss
~~Nothing~~ An endless ~~nothing.~~   ~~That this~~ will be ours
learn
Is what we ~~take from~~ here

nightly they try
~~bring at evening through the streets~~

propitiatory
With ~~pleading, worthless, frail~~
~~The~~ wasteful, weak, ~~propitiating~~ flowers.

He made some further unsuccessful attempts a week later:

When broken down, From here they can descry
Loss like a distant reef — loss, first of things,
Then loss of self, the deep vague frost of death
at random
Settling ~~on faces,~~ that on melting brings
~~That~~   theirs,
An endless absence. ~~All~~ This will be ~~ours~~ then ours
~~Is what we learn here~~ All comers learn
~~We learn by coming here~~

though each night many try

With wasteful, weak, propitiatory flowers

one
When broken down. From there ~~they~~ can descry
The end of life quite ~~easily~~ plainly
~~The distant reef approaching~~   ~~and lie still~~
~~Lest it see them~~

> When broken down. From there one can descry
> The end of life quite clearly. Those who leave
> cold
> Go knowing this, a small ~~chill~~ heavy thought
> Nothing will now dissolve

We again see here Larkin's proclivity to turn to figurative expression when having difficulty in bringing feeling into focus: "Loss like a far reef"; "the deep vague frost of death". Both figures would be eliminated later.

He returned to the poem on February 8th, completing it with the date "9 Feb 1972", which he circled. The circling may have been because he was dissatisfied. Immediately below the date he started redrafting his seventh stanza that began "Their separates from the cleaners—o world/Your loves . . . " He added, at the bottom of the page, a prose outline of what he wanted to do here—something unusual for him:

> Once moved from the outside world we see it as a touching
> dream to wch everyone is lulled, but ~~wch~~ from wch
> we awake when we get into hospital. In there is the
> only reality. There you see how transient and pointless everything
> in the world is Out there conceits and wishful thinking
> ~~and~~

On the following page he drafted his seventh stanza to the form that we know; but then appended a further note on the bottom of that page:

> That is what it means, this clean-sliced cliff, or
> rather it shows how great our wish is to deny its meaning,
> fear that
> higher than churches, for ~~if~~ nothing contravenes . . .

There is no further drafting of the poem in the Workbook; though this last prose note is close to the final conclusion of the poem. The final stanza, as he had left it earlier read:

> When broken down. All know they're going to die.
> perhaps not here
> Not yet, ~~not here, perhaps~~, but in the end,
> That is what ~~this~~ it means,
> And somewhere like this. ~~Nor will they forget~~
> and   ~~will~~
> This clean-sliced cliff, ~~and~~ what they / comprehend
> it

Long after they have left, ~~and~~ why it towers
Higher than churches. Nothing contravenes
                              ~~come~~ though many at evening
The coming dark, ~~those who nightly try~~   ~~dejected~~ try

With wasteful, weak, propitiatory flowers.

Evidently, once more, Larkin generated a typescript from his corrected text and made further revisions.

Throughout most of the drafting of "The Building" Larkin sets out a notation of his rhyme scheme beside his drafts. This often seems confusing, as the notation will begin, with the letter "A", part of the way down a stanza. If the rhyme scheme is examined stanza by stanza, it appears to be irregular. In fact, it is highly regular, though posing for Larkin a constricting task. The poem consists of nine seven-line stanzas, with a single final line standing alone. The rhyme scheme, "A/B/C/B/D/C/A/D" repeats every eight lines; so that its commencement shifts one line down the stanza with each new stanza. After eight stanzas, the conclusion of the rhyme scheme and the conclusion of the stanza coincide. In "The Building", as completed, this gives a final stanza in which the rhyme scheme and the stanza begin together, while the rhyme scheme is completed by the final line that stands alone. The effect of having "With wasteful, weak, propitiatory flowers" stand alone as the conclusion is to make the gesture of the flowers seem all the more vulnerable. Judging from Larkin's notation, the patterning was not clear with his first page of drafting, where he sets out the following scheme: "A/B/C/B/D/C/A [gap] D/E/F/G/F/H/G [gap] F/H"; though there is implied in this a linking of stanzas through the rhyme pattern. By this period of use of the notebooks, Larkin seems to have dated the top of the page on each new commencement of drafting; and, when he comes to the poem for his second attempt on Christmas Eve of 1971, he sets out "A/B/C/B/D/C [gap] A/D", where the notation begins with the second line of stanza two, and the gap corresponds to the gap between stanzas two and three. This corresponds to the pattern followed in the printed version, showing that, as was frequent with him, he hit on the rhyme scheme he was to use early in the drafting. This, of course, constituted a very tight commitment, if it was to be held to: the poem had either to be completed in exactly eight stanzas; or it had to have a stanza or stanzas with a loose line or lines at the end. The single line standing alone provided an elegant and effective solution; but making the narrative coincide in length with the demands of the rhyme scheme was a *tour de force*. As was seen, after drafting his first two-and-a-half stanzas, Larkin expanded them, so that some of the material already drafted emerged as late as the fifth stanza. Larkin had to make his material last, once he had adopted the rhyme scheme.

Heads in the Women's Ward

On pillow after pillow lies
The wild white hair and staring eyes;
Jaws stand open; necks are stretched
With every tendon sharply sketched;
A bearded mouth talks silently
To someone no one else can see.

Sixty years ago they smiled
At lover, husband, first-born child.

Smiles are for youth. For old age come
Death's terror and delirium.

"Heads in the Women's Ward" was drafted on the page immediately following "The Building", and is dated "6/3/72". Like "How", it was evidently written very rapidly:

On pillow after pillow lies
The wild white hair and staring eyes,
   Jaws ~~slack~~ stick
~~Mouths slack~~ open, necks are stretched,
With every tendon sharply etched,
~~And~~ ~~Or~~   talk
And ~~And~~ Bearded mouths ~~work~~ silently
         ~~visitors~~
   To ~~people~~   no one ~~else~~ can see
~~Bald stones on the beach of age.~~
      strangers   else

         ago
Sixty years ~~back~~ they smiled
~~On~~ At lover, husband, first-born child.

     self
Enjoy your ~~life~~   In old age
~~Take pride in youth.~~ ~~in age will~~ come
Death's terror and delirium.

Much of what is in "Heads in the Women's Ward" is taken up in "The Old Fools"; so that, although Larkin allowed the poem to be published in the *New Humanist* in May 1972, it is not surprising that he did not collect it in *High Windows* in 1974.

The Old Fools

What do they think has happened, the old fools,
To make them like this? Do they somehow suppose
It's more grown-up when your mouth hangs open and drools,
And you keep on pissing yourself, and can't remember
Who called this morning? Or that, if they only chose,
They could alter things back to when they danced all night,
Or went to their wedding, or sloped arms some September?
Or do they fancy there's really been no change,
And they've always behaved as if they were crippled or tight,
Or sat through days of thin continuous dreaming
Watching light move? If they don't (and they can't), it's strange:
        Why aren't they screaming?

At death, you break up: the bits that were you
Start speeding away from each other for ever
With no one to see. It's only oblivion, true:
We had it before, but then it was going to end,
And was all the time merging with a unique endeavour
To bring to bloom the million-petalled flower
Of being here. Next time you can't pretend
There'll be anything else. And these are the first signs:
Not knowing how, not hearing who, the power
Of choosing gone. Their looks show that they're for it:
Ash hair, toad hands, prune face dried into lines —
        How can they ignore it?

Perhaps being old is having lighted rooms
Inside your head, and people in them, acting.
People you know, yet can't quite name; each looms
Like a deep loss restored, from known doors turning,
Setting down a lamp, smiling from a stair, extracting
A known book from the shelves; or sometimes only
The rooms themselves, chairs and a fire burning,
The blown bush at the window, or the sun's
Faint friendliness on the wall some lonely
Rain-ceased midsummer evening. That is where they live:
Not here and now, but where all happened once.
        This is why they give

An air of baffled absence, trying to be there
Yet being here. For the rooms grow farther, leaving
Incompetent cold, the constant wear and tear

Of taken breath, and them crouching below
Extinction's alp, the old fools, never perceiving
How near it is. This must be what keeps them quiet:
The peak that stays in view wherever we go
For them is rising ground. Can they never tell
What is dragging them back, and how it will end? Not at night?
Not when the strangers come? Never, throughout
The whole hideous inverted childhood? Well,
                    We shall find out.

The drafting of "The Old Fools" commenced on September 12th, 1972. It began with a single line, "What do old people think is going on". This corresponds fairly closely to the opening line of the published poem, "What do they think has happened, the old fools". However, Larkin did not continue from that opening line, but turned, instead, to draft a different opening, "Look at that silly old sod trying to get on a bus". He made three shots at drafting an opening stanza; and, on September 14th, wrote out a fair copy of what he had done so far:

Look at that silly old fool trying to get on a bus.
He can't pull himself up, he's too gone at the knees.
Somebody shoves him: with a lot more fuss
He falls on a seat, and grins round like a kid,
Proud of being no use. Why does he think he's
Different now from when he played for the Works,
And old Mr. Fenton gave him five quid
                                    sort of
When they won the Shield? Does he think it's a ~~sort of~~ game
      his body won't do what
When ~~he can't understand~~ he wants, but dithers and jerks
To amuse the crowd?

Larkin also set out, beside the previous attempt at this stanza, the rhyme scheme that was followed in the poem. Then, on September 18th, he began drafting what was to be the opening stanza of the completed poem, returning to his original start with the line "What do they think has happened, the old fools". Very uncharacteristically, he abandoned the material of his initial opening, though the reference to playing cricket "for the Works" was kept in the initial drafting of the new opening; and the stanza pattern that had already emerged was adhered to. Possibly the original opening seemed too humorous; possibly Larkin preferred to begin with his stark and shocking question as his opening line. Whatever the reason, this abandonment of initial opening material was not a feature of other major long poems, such as "Church Going", "The Whitsun Weddings" or "The Building".

There is a diagram at the bottom of the first page of drafting from September 12th:

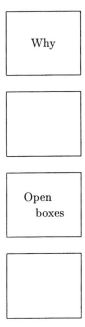

This seems to correspond to the pattern of the poem as completed, and to show that Larkin had a sense of the structure of the poem from the start. "Why" is the question posed in the opening stanza; while the "open boxes" emerge in the drafting of the third stanza, though transformed into "lighted rooms" in the final version.

The image of the old man climbing on to a bus is initially utilised in the new drafting:

> What do they think has happened, the old fools,
> When they can't walk straight, or climb on a waiting bus

This is quickly abandoned for the type of imagery encountered in "Heads in the Women's Ward": "if your mouth hangs open and drools". After two shots at the first three lines, in the second of which he departs from the already set rhyme scheme, Larkin returns to that rhyme scheme and completes the first stanza more or less as published.

What do they think has happened, the old fools,
                    Do they somehow suppose
To make them like this? ~~Don't they think it strange~~
It's better if your mouth hangs open and drools,
And you keep on pissing yourself, and can't remember
          saw
   Who ? ~~came~~ you ~~yesterday~~ or   only
~~What happened last week~~ / that if they / chose
          this morning:
They could alter it ~~all~~ to when they played for the Works,
                    back   ~~that~~ in
Or went to their wedding, or joined up ~~in~~ September?
          fancy ~~think~~   one
Or do they ~~believe~~ there really is no change   and
                         the ~~jumps and with their~~ shakes
          and ~~and~~ paper   ~~knee tremble~~ and
And the stick legs, ~~the sack of~~ skin, ~~the jerks~~ ~~furious~~ jerks
          passed in a thin continuous
And the days ~~that are like a constant tasteless~~ dreaming
   Were always like that   it's ~~rather~~ ~~surely~~ deeply
~~Are how they were always?~~ If not, ~~isn't it~~ / strange:
Why aren't they screaming?

A week later he made a fair copy of this version. The rhyming
words are the same as in the published version, with the exception
of the fifth and ninth lines, where the rhyme is "Works"/"jerks" in
contrast to the final "might"/"tight". The phrase "played for the
Works" is carried over from his rejected opening; but "the weak stiff
legs and paper skin, the shakes and jerks" belong to the new direction in tune with "Heads in the Women's Ward". These lines were
to undergo one change in later drafting; but most of the remaining
phrases of the published version are there, including the memorable
"days of thin continuous dreaming".

Before he made a fair copy, Larkin drafted the first five lines of the
second stanza:

At death, you break up, the things that were you
                    for ever
Start speeding away from each other, ~~in a dark~~
   With   Everyone
~~And there's~~ nothing left to watch them. ~~?~~   who
Remembers you dies as well. Every day
          this
Brings when ~~it~~ will happen nearer.

As frequently in passages of declarative statement, he writes quickly and clearly, getting his arrestingly direct first two lines more or less at first shot. In some respects, this illustrates a common feature of Larkin's writing in the increasingly complex stanza forms that he came to employ in his major poems. It is, indeed, inevitable that, further down a stanza, a writer finds himself hemmed in by his rhyme scheme; and a good deal of Larkin's drafting occurs at the end of stanzas and is devoted to getting tight and natural lines to fit the pre-arranged rhyme scheme.

After another incomplete attempt at the second stanza, Larkin returned to the poem a week later, on October 2nd, completing the stanza and beginning the third.

> At death you break up: the things that were you
> Start speeding away from each other for ever
> With nothing to watch them. Oblivion: True
> We had this before, but then it was all converging,
>   the whole
> Passing ~~everything in the~~ encyclopedia
>   a ~~the~~ the
> To burst into light, ~~the~~ million-petalled flower
>   the other
> Of being alive. This is ~~another~~ thing.
>   ~~are~~ get
> When you ~~get~~ near it, your hair grows thin and white,
>   you're so much
>   ~~have grown~~
>   They stop you working, because ~~you become~~ / slower,
> ~~They~~ send you   / When ~~If~~ you fail you're
> And ~~You go~~ for tests.   ~~To fail them will be~~   for it,
>   And lie watching the flicking tellyscreen light.
>   they
> ~~How~~ can you ignore it?

The pattern of the final version is there. However, many of the images are different. Somewhat obscurely, the period before birth is referred to as "Passing everything in the encyclopedia"; while the signs of age — "They stop you working, because you're so much slower,/They send you for tests" — are perhaps a little too comfortable for the tone of the poem.

Larkin then made a fair copy of his second stanza and moved on to draft the third stanza to completion:

                              dozens of
          ~~Perhaps~~ Being old is made up of// lighted boxes,
          Different and stuck together. They are acting in them.
          Bend down and watch: the man moving over the rocks is
                              shrimping
          Your father, carrying the ~~old~~ net; he turns,
          ~~And opens~~ Opening
          ~~Opening~~ / his mouth to speak. By some stratagem
          You are there, finding that thing in the sand, and try
          To hide it, when ~~that~~ this side of the room adjourns
          ~~Collapsing~~ By falling in, ~~like into becoming releasing expiring and~~
                                                        releasing

          ~~By falling inwards on to~~ / loving care.
                                        there's
          A curved movement, so soft, and ~~there is~~ the sky,
              The   that move
          ~~With~~ leaves ~~against it~~ and dip but always come back,
          ~~While light spreads along the~~ suddenly,   remembered face
            ~~They are there for hours intol~~, the intolerably face ~~?~~
          ~~The sun~~ hours
                  for/hours

Again, much that was there was not to survive into the final version.
The very evocative passage about "the man moving over the rocks"
is reminiscent of "To the Sea". Larkin is evidently attempting to
dramatise the rehearsal of the past that is taking place in the heads
of the Old Fools. He was to work on this, trying many variations, but
was ultimately to sacrifice the material for something more general.

   He then made a fair copy of the stanza, giving it the concluding
line:

    Is
    ~~A~~ now ending lack?

At the bottom of the page he adds what seems to be a sketch for the
conclusion of a stanza — a conclusion not taken up:

              continual
      Old age is ~~continuous~~
          ~~face of old age is~~
      ~~The faces of the old~~ are screaming
          Why can't you hear it?

   Two weeks later Larkin began work on the poem again, writing
out the second stanza and attempting a new conclusion to it. He did
not, however, reach the final line of the stanza. After that, he did

not return to the poem for over a month, and may have felt himself to be stuck. In the meantime, he made the following jottings on November 13th:

Death
Is something I'm scared of
I wish I could
By me daily
No good

Spare Time   Development

In the old days
I used to come home
And settle to ~~work~~ write
            famous   s
In the ~~thrilling~~ evenings.

Now I hit the jug
And go out like a light.
Waking, go to bed
With a hangover.

The last of these may have been expressive of his frustration. On the same page, he set out his rhyme scheme for "The Old Fools" again.

When he began once more on November 25th, Larkin wrote out the first two stanzas again, making extensive changes. The phrase "played for the Works", which had survived from his rejected opening, was now replaced by the rather clichéd "danced all night". As ever, it is a measure of Larkin's art that he could make such clichés emerge with telling appropriateness. The phrase "joined up in September" is replaced by "sloped arms in September" — not entirely felicitously: "sloped arms" is more physical than "joined up"; but it belongs to a cluster of drill movements — "port arms", "present arms", "order arms", so that it brings with it the unanswered question of why that particular movement is selected — a question that has no force for the poem. The rhyming words are now as in the published version. The redrafting had originally given "danced till dawn"; but, in working on the later rhyming line, Larkin hit on the image of the Old Fools staggering as though they were "tight", and must have gone back and changed "till dawn" to "all night".

Some conception of the detail of drafting that we encounter when Larkin is groping is seen in the work on the latter part of the second stanza:

> At death, you break up: the bits that were you
> Start speeding away from each other for ever
> With no one to watch. It's only oblivion, true:
> We had it before, but then it was ~~all~~ converging,
> ~~Orchestrating~~   incarnate orchestra
> ~~Collecting~~ The whole ~~orchestra~~ / of endeavour
> Coming   these are the
> ~~To come~~ to light, the million-petalled flower   first
>   ~~now you are~~
>   ~~all these~~
>   here ~~It's different now~~ Now it's different, a
> Of being ~~alive~~. ~~Now it's the opposite~~, merging and ~~these are the~~
>   ~~absence for evermore~~ to final absence ~~Watch out for~~
> To ~~widening absence~~. ~~Away finally~~, ~~These are the~~ signs:
>   how   who, not ~~doing having power to act~~   the
> Not knowing / not hearing / ~~not doing, not being able, not having~~
>   to run your own life gone. They mean you're   power
> ~~When things start not to work you know you're~~ for it.   for it
>   when
>   ~~When~~ You're going to die, / your face dries up in
> ~~Look at your face, dried up in eighty~~ / lines:
> Can you ignore it?   ignore can

The awkward phrase about "the whole encyclopedia" is replaced by an equally infelicitous metaphor the "whole incarnate orchestra of endeavour". In contrast, Larkin hits on a characteristic phrase of decided power and evocation in "widening absence". It does not stay; though it is to re-emerge in the final stanza as "baffled absence". Nonetheless, Larkin gets close to the final version of the stanza.

Four days later, Larkin made two attempts to redraft the third stanza, abandoning the seaside images for domestic ones — "mother sets down a lamp. There fire consumes/Something that remembering would rescue" — images closer to what he finally ended up with. In the second draft he tries out a tenderly evocative passage of disappointment, which was also to be lost in the final version:

> There they ~~all~~ are,
> Laughing under the trees, while at that desk you
> Write, and stare at the laurels.

Three days later, on December 1st, Larkin began redrafting the third stanza again, but abandoned it and wrote out from the beginning the whole poem so far, making several detailed changes to the conclusion of the second stanza — once again employing a characteristic way of getting back into a poem that is offering difficulties.

The following day, he made three more attempts at the early lines of the third stanza, again introducing new images that were later to be abandoned:

> Mother set down a lamp; Father consumes
> Whisky and the local weekly

At the conclusion of the page, he begins drafting the final stanza:

> An air of baffled absence, trying to be there
> Yet being here, where strangeness is, and pain,
>   Meantime
> And a sense of falling, ~~and~~ / the wear and tear
>   Of breathing breaks them down   much
>   ~~taking~~   ~~slowly~~ so ~~that~~   they miss
> ~~Of drawing breath tires them so much so they miss~~
>   Death's alp
> ~~The alp of death~~ at their elbow.

He gets no further than the fifth line; but his opening was to be his final version. On December 29th, he has two more shots at the third stanza, carefully setting out his rhyme scheme beside them. He drafts the whole stanza on his second attempt, arriving at a version close to the published one.

> Perhaps being old is having lighted rooms
> Inside your head, and people in them, acting.
> People you know, yet can't quite name: each looms
>   deep
>   a ~~great~~ loss restored
> Like ~~thankful restoration~~: from known doors turning,
>   from
>   smiling   ~~down~~ a passage
> Setting down a lamp, ~~beckoning from a chair~~, extracting
>   ~~only~~
> A known book from the shelves; or sometimes ~~there's~~ only
>   chairs and a
> The rooms themselves, ~~chairs watching the~~ fire burning,
>   ~~or~~ ~~and~~   sun's
> The blown bush at the window, or ~~and~~ the ~~wall~~
>   on the wall ~~that~~ some
> ~~When sun's~~ Ḟaint friendliness ~~after rain in a~~ lonely
> Rainceased   where they live
> ~~Rainwet~~ midsummer evening. ~~in~~ This is ~~what they see~~ s,
>   where all
> Not here and now, but ~~all that~~ happened once:

                    This is why they give
                    ~~These are what they give~~

Finally, on January 11th, he made a fair version of the stanza almost
as published.

As so frequently in his longer poems, the passages in the poem that
give Larkin the most trouble are the ones where the poem is about
to bring its meaning into focus, prior to precipitating its conclusion.
This was seen in "Church Going" and in "The Whitsun Weddings". In
this poem less work is devoted at this point to trying out figurative
expressions than in the drafting of the earlier poems. Rather it is
spent on finding detail appropriately evocative for its moment in the
poem.

Once Larkin had his third stanza concluded, he took up the three
or four lines of the final stanza that he had written and completed the
stanza the next day in one go, though with many corrections. Once
again, he set out the rhyme scheme at the side of the page as a guide.

        An air of baffled absence, trying to be there
        Yet being here. For the rooms grow fainter, leaving
        Incompetent cold, the constant wear and tear
        Of taken breath, and them crouching below
                            ~~without~~ the old fools ~~not~~ never
        Extinction's ~~towering~~ alp ~~of being dead and not~~ perceiving
        The ~~vast~~ invisible alp of death.   /
                near   must be ~~why~~ what keeps
        ~~What's there closeWhat standsHow near it is. Why~~ keeps ~~the eye~~
                                                                    them
        ~~How near it is: / so near.~~ That's ~~how they show fairly~~ quiet
        ~~Because this~~   ~~stares at follows us that always?~~
                    ~~that rises we can't lose that follows us~~
        The peak ~~that sails in front sight of~~ /   wherever we go ~~?~~
                \that stays in view/   can ~~Do~~ they never
                                ~~So they never wonder Don't they ever~~
        For them is rising ground.   ~~making them stumble guess~~ tell
                                                how
        What's dragging them back, and ~~where~~ it will end? Not at night?
                        ~~it is all~~ the
        Not when ~~there's no one but~~ strangers come? Never throughout
        The whole hideous inverted childhood?   Well,
                    We shall find out
                    ~~So late in the day.~~

There is no fair copy of the final stanza; but inspection of the corrections shows that little change was made when the poem was put into typescript. The poem is dated "12.1.73".

The focusing metaphor of the "peak", taken as in "The Whitsun Weddings" from the general poetic stock rather than from the world of the poem, appeared in the first attempt at the final stanza on December 12th as "Death's alp at their elbow". In the next two sketches of the stanza, Larkin did not reach that line; but in the final version it re-emerges first as "The peak that sails in front", then "that we can't lose sight of", and finally as "that stays in view". The last four lines of the drafting appear to have come with relative ease; but, even if Larkin had a conclusion in mind, the final surprising inversion seems to have been a last correction.

"How" and "Heads in the Women's Ward" are not insignificant poems, even though they were written very rapidly, while "The Building" and "The Old Fools" involved extensive drafting. The speed with which a poem is written has never been a measure of its quality. What took time with longer poems was the extensive orchestration of detail. This orchestration, as in "The Whitsun Weddings", had a realist, novelistic quality: it did not aim at a structure of metaphor or metaphorical detail; though the "building" itself is given an awsome metaphorical quality through much of the detail. In these respects, the drafting of the two longer poems was very characteristic of Larkin's work.

Chapter 10

SHORTER AND SATIRICAL POEMS

In contrast with Larkin's longer poems, some of his shorter poems indeed came very quickly. This was particularly true of his satirical poems. An example is "Wires".

Wires

The widest prairies have electric fences,
For though old cattle know they must not stray
Young steers are always scenting purer water
Not here but anywhere. Beyond the wires

Leads them to blunder up against the wires
Whose muscle-shredding violence gives no quarter.
Young steers become old cattle from that day,
Electric limits to their widest senses.

"Wires" came in one shot:

The widest prairies have e~~l~~éctric fences
For   old
~~For~~ though ~~the~~ cattle ~~k~~now they must not stray
                    scenting
Young steers are a~~l~~ways ~~glimpsing~~ purer water
              any~~w~~here
More tender ~~there~~   ~~world~~
Not here but ~~Or fresher~~ gra~~ss/~~ a ~~That wish~~ Beyond the wires

Leads them to blunder up against the wires,
Whose m~~u~~scle-shredding agony gives no quarter.
Young steers become old cattle from that day;
    Ele~~c~~tric ~~wire-staked~~ ~~round~~ their widest senses.
~~The widest prairies have electric fences.~~
              limits   to

It is annotated "Before breakfast 4/xi/50". The poem is structured so that the lines of the first stanza rhyme in reverse with those of the second stanza. Larkin begins this mirroring by having the fourth and the fifth lines end in the same word, "wires" (the title of the poem).

The entire drafting is given of all the poems discussed in this chapter, except that of "Broadcast".

The only major change is to the last line — initially the same as the
first line. The change may possibly have been made because having
the first and last lines of the stanzas the same might have given the
poem a circularity rather than a conclusion.

However, shortness did not always go along with rapid drafting.
Another satirical poem, "Send No Money", which Larkin described
as "the one I repeat to myself",[1] was worked on from September 27th
1960 to November 11th through twenty pages of the Workbook. It was
then set aside and returned to on August 10th 1962 and completed in
ten days with a further two pages of drafting. In contrast, the entire
composition of the very similar "Study of Reading Habits", written
shortly before "Send No Money" was begun, took a page and a half.

Wild Oats

About twenty years ago
Two girls came in where I worked —
A bosomy English rose
And her friend in specs I could talk to.
Faces in those days sparked
The whole shooting-match off, and I doubt
If ever one had like hers:
But it was the friend I took out,

And in seven years after that
Wrote over four hundred letters,
Gave a ten-guinea ring
I got back in the end, and met
At numerous cathedral cities
Unknown to the clergy. I believe
I met beautiful twice. She was trying
Both times (so I thought) not to laugh.

Parting, after about five
Rehearsals, was an agreement
That I was too selfish, withdrawn,
And easily bored to love.
Well, useful to get that learnt.
In my wallet are still two snaps
Of bosomy rose with fur gloves on.
Unlucky charms, perhaps.

"Wild Oats", originally "Love Life", was written in three days,
10th, 11th and 12th of May 1962, and there are two drafts, with
alterations to each. The first draft is of the first and second stanzas

and the concluding lines of the third; the second draft is of the whole
poem.

Love Life

About twenty years ago
Two girls came in where I worked: /—
A bosomy "English rose"
And
~~With~~ ~~And~~ one in specs I could talk to/
~~Theologies~~In those days, faces sparked
~~Whole ontologies~~
~~Theologies~~ Aesthetiques off, and I doubt/   one
        ~~If any did more than~~ If ~~one~~ ever /did like hers.
        ~~If one ever did like hers:~~
                    her ~~second~~ ~~shortsighted~~ friend
        But I took ~~the other one out:~~ one out
            ~~the second one I took~~
                        weak-eyed

And In   For   after that
        ~~In~~ seven years, ~~I suppose,~~
                her four hundred letters
        ~~We wrote /~~ ~~all the right~~   ~~each~~
            ~~saw the~~ Bought her a cheap ring
        ~~?~~   ~~cathedral cities~~
    I got back in the end/~~sent back~~ and stayed at
        ~~(Which she returned)~~   ~~We stayed~~
                    ~~returned~~
        ~~All~~ Certain
        ~~Saw the~~ cathedral cities
                        I met
        The other /
        ~~I met~~   /one twice.   She seemed
        To be trying not to laugh.

                In my wallet
                    ~~two snaps~~ I keep
        Two snaps of her in the snow.
        ~~I look at them sometimes~~
        More for luck than anything.
        That's the past for you.

It is interesting that in this first draft, Larkin does not carry the drafting through stanza by stanza, or line by line; he gives himself the clinching target conclusion of the "snaps" in the wallet before he has attempted to draft the intervening lines. This was not his usual procedure; though in this poem, the ironic twist at the end is almost the *raison d'être* of the piece. Larkin did indeed remark that "I used to find that I was never sure I was going to finish a poem until I had thought of the last line . . . But usually the last line would come when I'd done about two-thirds of the poem, and then it was just a matter of closing the gap".[2] This seems to be the only documented example of his doing this.

Characteristically, Larkin finds his rhyme scheme in the first stanza and stays with it. The remainder of the drafting consists in fitting the poem to that scheme. Certain of the details that are important in stanza two — the "ring", the "cathedral cities", and "beautiful" trying not to laugh — are already there; but the phrasing had to be adjusted to the form of the poem and for reasons of tone. The one item that he did not have in the first draft was the "parting" that led into the conclusion. This emerged in the second and final draft.

<u>Love Life</u>

```
        About twenty years ago
            A girl
Two girls Two girls came in where I worked/-/ —
    With    A bosomy "English rose"
  And a   With a friend
   And    And one in specs I could talk to.
          In those days, faces sparked
No end All the usual
sorts of stuffCosmologies off, and I doubt
            any did more than
        If ever one did like hers:
            it was the friend
        But the second one I took out/,

            in
        And for
        And the seven years after that/
          I Wrote about
  I    I Wrote her four hundred letters,
            a ten guinea
        Bought her a cheap ring
        I got back in the end, and stayed at
```

Certain cathedral cities
                              ~~I met~~ In brief
Without blessing of clergy.   ~~?~~   ~~?~~
        Beautiful   She was
I met   ~~The other girl~~ twice.   ~~She was~~   trying
                                          ~~giggle~~
Both times (so I thought) not to ~~laugh~~ laugh.

    The parting
    ~~We parted~~
~~We parted~~ after about five
            was ~~general~~ the
Rehearsals,   in ~~the~~ / agreement
                      cold
That I was too selfish, ~~and cruel~~ repressed
And easily bored for love.
                              useful
        ~~good to get~~ ~~something~~ /   get
That was ~~all I learnt~~   / to ~~have~~ learnt.
            are ~~still have~~ small
In my wallet   ~~I keep~~   two / snaps
  ~~My wallet still carries~~
                      ~~against~~ well muffled.
Of bosomy Rose, ~~in the / snow out of doors/~~
~~Kept as~~ Unlucky charms/,perhaps.
                              12.5.62

In the light of all the work expended on the second draft, it is
worth noting that what Larkin originally wrote for his first stanza,
before making any alterations, is very close to the printed version:

Love Life	Wild Oats
1 About twenty years ago	About twenty years ago
2 Two girls came in where I worked: —	Two girls came in where I worked
3 A bosomy "English rose"	A bosomy English rose
4 And one in specs I could talk to.	And her friend in specs I could talk to.
5 In those days faces sparked	Faces in those days sparked
6 Aesthetiques off, and I doubt	The whole shooting match off, and I doubt
7 If one ever did like hers.	If ever one had like hers:
8 But I took the other one out.	But it was the friend I took out.

The original attempts at lines 1, 2 and 3 are the same as in the printed version. Line 5 is the same, except for an inversion of "In those days" and "faces"; and 7 is the same except that "had" was later substituted for "did" and there is an inversion of "one" and "ever". The rather jaunty movement of the poem is there, as is the phrasing that leads to the isolated, ironic concluding line. Line 6 has more syllables in the final version; and that irregularity makes the movement feel more natural.

Yet Larkin, in working on his first draft, crossed out line 7 and tried two variations on it. He tried a further variation in the second draft; but came back close to the original in the end. "And" at the beginning of line 3 is replaced by "With" in the first draft, and again in the second draft; but "And" is reinstated both times. Such changes, leading to the conclusion that the first attempt was best, account for much of Larkin's re-drafting, here as elsewhere.

Breadfruit

Boys dream of native girls who bring breadfruit,
   Whatever they are,
As brides to teach them how to execute
Sixteen sexual positions on the sand;
This makes them join (the boys) the tennis club,
Jive at the Mecca, use deodorants, and
On Saturdays squire ex-schoolgirls to the pub
   By private car.

Such uncorrected visions end in church
   Or registrar:
A mortgaged semi- with a silver birch;
Nippers; the widowed mum; having to scheme
With money; illness; age. So absolute
Maturity falls, when old men sit and dream
Of naked native girls who bring breadfruit
   Whatever they are.

"Breadfruit", written about six months before "Wild Oats", was worked over on only one page of the Workbook, though rather extensively.

~~Men are all alike~~
<u>Breadfruit</u>

native
~~naked~~
~~naked~~ girls
~~sand and~~

Boys dream of ~~islands~~ who bring breadfruit,   A
     to   teach them how
~~{~~Whatever they are~~)~~,   ~~how to~~ ~~for being taught~~ to   B
   As bribes   ~~for learning with~~
~~To bribe you into showing them, and execute~~ execute   A
Sixteen sexual positions on the sand/;   C
which   ~~Thunder of surf, morning and evening star,~~
makes them   ~~sleep~~   ~~fresh~~
    ~~Rough wine, roast pig, ? and then more girls again~~
~~Therefore~~ they then join ~~them in~~   (the boys) ~~join~~ the
This makes ~~This search out ?~~ ~~join the local~~ tennis club   D
     use
     Mecca   ~~with~~ ~~buy~~ deodorants,   and
Jive at the ~~Palais,~~ ~~makes wander hand in hand~~   C
On   ~~take~~ ex schoolgirls ~~to~~
~~Each~~ Saturdays ~~see~~ ~~half stewed girls home~~ nights to
~~With girls they take~~   ~~drive home~~ from the pub   D
   ~~run~~   By private
\squire/   In ~~?~~   car.   B

~~Clutching some~~
~~Grasping at this, he~~
~~These Immature visions lead to morning suit~~
     ~~And cheap cigar,~~
   ~~The mortgaged villa nippers~~

       in   church
Such uncorrected visions end ~~in~~ ~~with ring~~
~~Immature longings, lead to parish church~~   A
    or   ~~And~~ ~~or~~ registrar,
     ~~And cheap cigar~~   B
     with a silver birch,   A
A mortgaged semi-   ~~nippers, illness,~~
     mum   having
Nippers, a widowed ~~in-law,~~ ~~the need~~ to scheme   C
With ~~For~~ money, illness; age, till absolute   D
~~To make ends meet, illness,~~
Maturity reigns. Then old men sit and dream   C
Of naked native girls bringing breadfruit,   D
    Whatever they are.   B
     19.xi.61

This brief, satirical poem, with all its workings set out in one draft, illustrates the extent to which composing a poem of this type was like solving a puzzle for Larkin. Here there is little pressure for sensitive verbal articulation of feeling. Larkin evidently at first intended to expand the initial vision of "native girls", but turned to the real consequences of the vision, deleting his first attempt. At some point he must have come to the idea of having a poem of two stanzas, with a conclusion that circled back to the opening phrase, thus mirroring the entrapment that the poem speaks of. This is evidenced by the fact that the last two lines are subject to no correction — in contrast with the opening lines of the second stanza, which constitute the turning point of the poem. It was a matter of making something of the material within the structure adopted — and, of course, of making the structure do something for the material. "Breadfruit" was not collected by Larkin. It was published in *Critical Quarterly* for Winter 1964. That version follows the Workbook in having "bribes" in the third line. *Collected Poems* has "brides".

Naturally the Foundation will Bear Your Expenses

Hurrying to catch my Comet
    One dark November day,
Which soon would snatch me from it
    To the sunshine of Bombay,
I pondered pages Berkeley
    Not three weeks since had heard,
Perceiving Chatto darkly
    Through the mirror of the Third.

Crowds, colourless and careworn,
    Had made my taxi late,
Yet not till I was airborne
    Did I recall the date —
That day when Queen and Minister
    And Band of Guards and all
Still act their solemn-sinister
    Wreath-rubbish in Whitehall.

It used to make me throw up,
    These mawkish nursery games:
O when will England grow up?
    — But I outsoar the Thames,
And dwindle off down Auster
    To greet Professor Lal
(He once met Morgan Forster),
    My contact and my pal.

The drafting of "Naturally the Foundation will Bear Your Expenses" gives an unusual insight into the way Larkin worked in his satirical poems. It was begun on November 14th 1960. The following reproduces, as nearly as possible, the first page:

14.11.60   from it

~~My pigskin bags and I~~
~~On our way to the Air Terminal~~
~~The day I~~
~~Hurrying to catch my Comet~~ | grow up |
~~My pigskin bags and I~~ | throw up |

                          a
~~Hurrying to catch my Comet~~
~~To take me to Bombay~~

                          ~~Cenotaph~~

          ~~I could not help but laugh~~
damp   I went
~~dank~~   ~~Hurrying~~
on a ~~dark~~   ~~Hurrying~~ to catch a comet
     ~~rain~~   ~~one~~ November day
~~One dull~~   ~~Upon Remembrance Day~~
                  ~~And~~ soon wd ~~take me~~ snatch me from it
     (Which   ~~Which when I landed from it~~
To the sunlight ~~I should be~~ of
~~Would leave me~~ ~~Would leave me~~ in Bombay
                        polished
     ?~~caring~~   ~~I mused on~~
I carried   ~~To give this~~ talks that Berkeley
                        month
The month before ~~Only last week~~ had heard,
                    Perceiving Chatto
          ~~And I could see~~ Faber darkly ~~Chatto~~
     ~~Through the mirror of~~
                ~~After being in~~ The Third
          ~~Next in line behind~~
                Through the mirror of

The composition is clearly dominated by the setting up of the pattern of comic rhymes. The words "from it", at the top of the page, are noted as a possible rhyme for Comet; while the first full attempt covers the eight lines of a stanza, but is mainly space: Larkin saw that "Cenotaph" would rhyme with "laugh" and placed the words in what he thought might be their position, intending then to fill up the spaces. In fact he did not use this pair of words as rhymes; while the boxed "grow up" and "throw up", noted with the same purpose, were not to be used until the third stanza.

The narrative leads Larkin along; though there are some rapid changes of direction, even in mid-sentence. Notable is "After being in" that is followed by "The Third". Clearly Larkin thought of periodical publication preceding a book as he wrote the first part of the line; but, as soon as the rhyme with "heard" had given him "The Third" (the B.B.C. Third Programme), he deleted his opening phrase. The rhyming words were here discovered as the poem went along; but the narrative of the poem was fitted to them as soon as they arrived.

The following day Larkin copied out his first stanza, making many alterations:

> my
> Hurrying to catch ~~a~~ comet
> ~~On a~~
> ~~One~~ damp November day
> ~~Which was booked to~~ thank God wd
> Which(~~It soon would~~ snatch me from it
> shine
> sun~~light~~
> To the ~~wisdom of~~ Bombay)
> I ~~proof read~~   ~~pondered lines~~   ~~clipped the~~ pages
> pondered   ~~I carried talks that~~ / Berkeley
> \\~~pondered~~/   ~~shuffled~~ once
> not   A   \ on   /
> Three ~~not~~   ~~The month~~ ago had heard
> weeks   ~~fancied~~
> Perceiving   ~~And could see~~ Chatto darkly
> Through the mirror of the Third.

As can be seen, many of the changes led back to what had already been arrived at, as was so often the case with Larkin's alterations.

He then proceeded to his second stanza:

> ~~And~~ ~~Not till we were airborne~~
> ~~think~~ recall the date
> Did I ~~recall it had been~~
>
> careworn
> Of cenotaph and Queen
> ~~Surround the Cenotaph~~
> And Ministers and

```
                    colourless
    Crowds     Dumb and
    Quiet      Crowds quiet and careworn
         Had
    Crowds     Nearly made me late
         But
         And   Not till we were airborne
               Did I recall the date.
```

Here, unusually, after beginning the stanza with lines built round the rhymes "airborne" and "careworn", he reverses the rhymes and the lines.

Larkin stopped at this point. What intervened was the writing of "Ambulances". He did not return to the poem until January 22 1961.

From London Far

Hurrying to catch my Comet
One dark November day,
Which soon wd snatch me from it
To the sunshine of Bombay,
I pondered pages Berkeley
        since
Not three weeks ~~ago~~ had heard
Perceiving Chatto darkly
Through the mirror of the Third.

```
             Crowds, colourless and careworn
    Had                    me
      /Nearly made my taxi late,
             Yet not till we were airborne
             Did I recall the date —
             The day when Queen and Minister
             And Band of Guards and all
                          their
             Act out        a solemn -
Still Act    Played out the simple-sinister
                          rubbish
               Wreath-anties
             Nursery anties in Whitehall.
                          It used
             It They it once it wd make me
             It's enough to make you throw up,
                          mawkish
               Going These anniversary nursery games
             Such in year after year
```

> will
> (O, when ~~is~~ England ~~going to~~ grow up?)
> ~~I soar above the Thames~~
> ~~And sink them in the Thames?~~ Now I outsoar the Thames
> ~~Dwindling away on Auster~~ Dwindling away on
> ~~And dwindle off on Auster~~ ~~And dwindle off on Auster~~
> To ~~the hopes~~———~~of~~ stay with
>   here
> ~~But there was~~ / Chandrie Lal
>   met
> (He once ~~knew~~ Morgan Forster),
>   contact
> My ~~chairman~~ and my pal./
>   23/1/61

Once again, the rhyming words are held to, while the phrasing is tuned up. With the line about Auster, Larkin swings back and forth, rather characteristically, between two very similar choices.

In the drafting of this comic poem, we see Larkin exploring its possibilities in terms of sets of comic rhymes, whose position he initially identifies. This approach is not encountered in the drafting of his non-comic poems, where, in contrast, phrases are often developed independently of the requirements of the rhyme scheme and then are fitted to it.

Home is so Sad

> Home is so sad. It stays as it was left,
> Shaped to the comfort of the last to go
> As if to win them back. Instead, bereft
> Of anyone to please, it withers so,
> Having no heart to put aside the theft
>
> And turn again to what it started as,
> A joyous shot at how things ought to be,
> Long fallen wide. You can see how it was:
> Look at the pictures and the cutlery.
> The music in the piano stool. That vase.

"Home is so Sad", a more characteristic and decided triumph, occupies only one and a half pages in the work-book. It was evidently begun on 29th December 1958 and completed the following day. Its initial startling phrase is there at the first shot:

> ~~Home is so sad when you are grown and gone~~
>
> ~~When you leave home~~

The phrase no doubt arose from Larkin's reaction to Christmas, then recently passed with his mother; though the qualifying adverbial clause in this initial drafting mutes the shock that the opening phrase has for some in the final version, where it is grammatically isolated. It takes Larkin a couple more shots to get to the opening as we have it:

> Home is so sad. It cannot shrink to size
> When you are grown and gone. It stays stretched out
>
> Home is so sad. It stays as it was left.
>   the carpet bleached in squares
> Furniture kicked, not matching
> Under the window

The images of deterioration go in the next attempt; where Larkin tries out many phrases before he arrives at something close to the final version, " shaped to the wishes of the ones who go". The remainder of the first stanza comes easily, and the rhyme scheme is established, with the rhyming words that remain with the poem.

> Home is so sad. It stays as it was left
> Shaped The shape of those who go
>   ?   shaped to please the ones who
>   Keeping the shape of wishes long   ?   have gone
> Shaped to please those who go   ?   outgrown
>   shaped to the wishes of the ones who go
>   else
> In case To they should come back; Or is it that, bereft
>   somebody
>   anyone
> Of wishes / to please

> Home is so sad. It stays as it was left,
>   the
>   those last to
> Shaped to the wishes of the ones who go,
> As if they might come back. + Or else, bereft
>   it
> Of somebody to please, they withers so,
>   will
>   Not having heart ? heart to palliate
> Having no Its purpose fallen   ?   put aside   the theft
>   ?   put aside

The second stanza also came easily, the majority remaining as drafted with little change.

　　　going　　　　　　　started as:
By ~~turning~~ back to what it ~~was at first:~~
　　A
~~The~~ joyous shot at how things ought to be,
Long fallen wide. How out of date ~~of date~~ it was.
Look at the pictures and the cutlery,
　　　　　　　　　　~~a~~ That vase.
The music in the piano stool, ~~the~~ vase.
　　　　　　　　　　~~the~~
　　　　　　　　　30.xii.58

This draft, which appears to be the penultimate draft, is very close to the final poem. However, on the next page, apparently intending to make a fair copy, Larkin makes several attempts to rewrite the second line of the first stanza and the first half of the third, only to come back, rather characteristically, to something close to what he already had. He tries "Suiting" for "shaped to"; but the only change that is adopted is "comfort" in place of "wishes". He even goes back to those opening lines after he has dated the poem, only to give up, evidently concluding, as so often, that his first thoughts were the best.

Home Is So Sad

　　　Home is so sad. It stays as it was left,
~~Suiting~~ the　　~~Keeping~~ the ~~wishes comfort~~ comfort
~~Shaped to~~ ~~Shaped to the wishes~~ of the last to go
~~Perhaps to~~ ~~call them they might come~~
　　　　　　　　~~to win them~~
　　　~~As if they might come~~ back. Or else, bereft
　　　~~As if they might come~~ to bring them
　　　Of somebody to please, it withers so
　　　　Having no
　　　~~Without the~~ heart to put aside the theft
　　　　~~going~~
And turn ~~By turning back~~ to what it
　again　~~And be again the place~~
　　　~~By going back to what it~~ started as,
　　　A joyous shot at how things ought to be,
　　　　　　　　You can see how
　　　Long fallen wide. ~~How ordinary~~ it was:
　　　Look at the pictures, and the cutlery.
　　　The music in the piano stool. That vase.

　　　　　　31 xii 58

Home is so sad. It stays as it was left,
Shaped to the comfort of the last to go
As if to bring them back

Later, when he prepared a typescript, Larkin typed "Suiting to", but changed it in handwriting back to "Shaped to".

The poem comes alive when Larkin hits on one of his glorious aphorisms: "A joyous shot at how things ought to be,/Long fallen wide". He makes no attempt to change this; and it fixes the tone of the poem. The early images had already been dropped, so that the poem became a series of imageless remarks for ten of its twelve lines. This in fact makes the images with which it closes have a static, almost ossified quality, in keeping with the statement in the first line.

Two of Larkin's tenderest poems, "Dublinesque" and "Broadcast", both came with comparatively little drafting— "Dublinesque" with almost none at all.

Dublinesque

Down stucco sidestreets,
Where light is pewter
And afternoon mist
Brings lights on in shops
Above race-guides and rosaries,
A funeral passes.

The hearse is ahead,
But after there follows
A troop of streetwalkers
In wide flowered hats,
Leg-of-mutton sleeves,
And ankle-length dresses.

There is an air of great friendliness,
As if they were honouring
One they were fond of;
Some caper a few steps,
Skirts held skilfully
(Someone claps time),

And of great sadness also.
As they wend away
A voice is heard singing
Of Kitty, or Katy,
As if the name meant once
All love, all beauty.

In Dublin's back streets/
    the
Where / light is pewter/
      afternoon fog
And ~~racing editions~~
~~And holy images~~
  Brings lights   ~~to~~ on in
~~Are ? sold in the~~ shops
The little shops.
A funeral passes.

    hearse   ahead
The ~~front~~ is ~~out of sight~~
    after   follows
But ~~behind~~ there ~~walk~~
  A troop
~~Some dozen~~ of street-walkers
   antique
In ~~great flowered~~ hats
And leg of mutton sleeves
And ankle length dresses.

There is
~~They leave~~
  ~~There is~~ an air of great friendliness,
As if they were honouring
         were
Someone they ~~are~~ fond of:
Some caper a few steps,
    held   ~~dancing~~
~~?~~ Skirts ~~swirling dance~~ skilfully
~~Time is beaten~~
~~A drum beats   somewhere~~
(Someone ~~beats~~ time).
      claps

     great
And of sadness also.
  ~~Away down the alleys~~
~~As well as the dance~~ As they wind away
   A voice is heard singing
~~Someone sings a song~~
  Of
~~About~~ 'Kitty' or 'Katy'
~~once~~ the name   ~~held for them~~
As if /   ~~Who for them summarised~~ meant for them
All love, all beauty.   6/6/70

The page on which the drafting began is headed "1.6.70"; the second
page, "6.6.70", indicating that the poem was probably completed in
two attempts. The first page has some deleted lines above those
quoted:

> ~~It will not change, now I am~~
> ~~To grow older is to see which lines rub out~~
>   deepen
> ~~Which harden into~~

If related in theme to the poem, they do not seem part of it.

Only a very few changes were made when Larkin typed the poem
out. The ease with which so much felicity was attained may in part
be due to the fact that "Dublinesque" is not in a rhyming form, which
was also true of "Days", another poem of remarkable stillness, which
came with little drafting. As already noted, Larkin's intense drafting
of some poems arises from attempts to accommodate his material to
rhyme, rather than letting the rhyme lead him to the material.

Broadcast

Giant whispering and coughing from
Vast Sunday-full and organ-frowned-on spaces
Precede a sudden scuttle on the drum,
'The Queen', and huge resettling. Then begins
A snivel on the violins:
I think of your face among all those faces,

Beautiful and devout before
Cascades of monumental slithering,
One of your gloves unnoticed on the floor
Beside those new, slightly-outmoded shoes.
Here it goes quickly dark. I lose
All but the outline of the still and withering

Leaves on half-emptied trees. Behind
The glowing wavebands, rabid storms of chording
By being distant overpower my mind
All the more shamelessly, their cut-off shout
Leaving me desperate to pick out
Your hands, tiny in all that air, applauding.

"Broadcast" was begun on November 5th 1961 and completed the
following day. Larkin described it being "about as near as I get
. . . to a love poem."[3] This tender poem was evidently completed
just thirteen days before the sexually iconoclastic "Breadfruit", and

appears immediately before it in Workbook No. 6. It was occasioned by Larkin's hearing on the radio a concert that Maeve Brennan was attending in Hull.[4]

The drafting begins unusually with what was to become, with one small change, the last line of the poem — again, one of the few occasions when Larkin sets out his final line and then goes about "closing the gap":[5]

> tiny
> Your tiny hands, / in that huge space applauding

This no doubt encapsulates the impulse for the poem — listening to a concert with the knowledge that, somewhere in the applause, he is hearing the clapping of someone he loves.

After a few shots, he arrives at an opening line: "The giant whispering and coughing". This leads into a passage in which "serious music" (as it was then termed) is given derogatory treatment characteristic of the Movement poems of a few years earlier:

> from
> Giant whispering and coughing ~~from~~
> ~~Th~~ast sunday-full and organ-frowned-on spaces
>   a
> Precedes ~~the~~ sudden scuttle on the drum,
> ~~Finds me alone~~
>   ~~the settling down again~~
> "The Queen", the ? / ? ? ~~the settling down~~
>   huge
>   A   and ~~the~~ ~~?~~ resettling; then begins
> ~~The first~~ snivel on the violins.
> I think of your face among all those faces.

The tellingly simple and touching last line of this passage came as it was to stay.

The drafting continues with the unironic treatment of his feelings for the woman: "Beautiful and devout" beside the ironic characterisation of the music as "slithering"; though the ironic and the unironic come together, touchingly, in the details of the "outmoded shoes" and "One of your gloves unnoticed on the floor". Although the phrasing is subject to some heavy drafting, the key images of the poem are arrived at without groping — the "gloves", the "shoes", the "withering leaves" outside. Larkin takes the poem almost to its conclusion; but then is halted, characteristically, by the problem of finding his way to that conclusion, even though he has his final line:

Fair haired and devout
Beautiful and devout and dark
            before
Beautiful and devout and dark
  That shapeless orchestrated
That The orchestra's impressive slitherings,
  One of your gloves unnoticed on the floor
    Beside   new   dated outmoded
LyingLies by your new; slightly outmoded shoes.
                              the
    Outside   Here it is nearly dark; and withering
  Here it is The leaves have finished withering
    Leaves   hang few and
  Outside   are   thinly   yellow
    Remaining leaves outside are yellow
Leaves still left hang yellow   Wa Watching, I lose
        outside

                    and
  The thread of my impatience, till

The next day he transcribed what he had done in a fair version;
and the first section of the poem was subject to further changes in
the process. The rhyme scheme, already established in the drafting
of the first stanza, is set out beside the draft of the third stanza.
While there is again much reworking of the second stanza, Larkin
stays with the rhyming words of his first version. The fourth line
of that stanza is dickered with extensively, no doubt in an effort to
get the tone right; but what emerges as the final version— "Beside
those new, slightly-outmoded shoes" — is very little different from
what Larkin transcribed when he began this second draft— "Beside
your new slightly outmoded shoes". This in turn is the same as what
he first wrote down, except for the word "Beside". Once again, we
see him coming back to first thoughts after much redrafting.

  It was the last stanza that gave the most trouble.

    Leaves in half-emptied   trees. Behind   A
    The thread of
                    the rising storms of chording   B
    The glowing wavebands music storms, affording
Free of Prove   What's the what's
    Proof that what's out of sight is more in mind   A
    Unhindered by   C
                              hear
        And leaves me trying to pick out   C

~~in all that~~
~~Your hands, tiny in that~~   ~~applauding~~.   B

---

     of
Leaves ~~in~~ half-emptied trees. Behind
The glowing wavebands, rising storms of chording
~~Show~~ ~~Assume more completely~~ my take a more hold
Take hold more easily
~~Prove the unseen shakes the~~ unhindered mind
          till the end shocks like a shout
For ~~By~~ being unseen, ~~ending with a~~
     ~~To leave~~ leaving
~~And leaves~~ me trying to pick out
Your hands,   , applauding.

He gets, at his first attempt, the phrase that will be the basis for the transition to his conclusion — "And leaves me trying"; but then seems dissatisfied with the very effective final line with which work on the poem started.

He attempts a fair version of the poem on the next page, making no more changes to the first two stanzas, except to cross out a comma; and these stanzas are as in the printed version, except that "goes" was later substituted for "grows", not affecting the tonal quality of its line. However, the third stanza is again worked over heavily, principally in the lines that became "rabid storms of chording/By being distant overpower my mind/All the more shamelessly, their cut-off shout".

Leaves of half-emptied trees. Behind
         ~~pulsing~~ rising
The glowing wavebands ~~spring~~ storms of chording
      By being out of sight
     ~~By being out of sight~~   assume my
     ~~Flood more completely my unwilling~~ mind
Utterly   ~~Completely~~   ~~breaking~~ ~~boiling to~~ their shrilling ending shout
         ~~flooding like a liquid shout~~
     ~~By being unseen shrilling~~
       ~~That leaves~~
Leaving ~~To leave~~ me ~~me~~ trying to pick out
Your hands, tiny in all that air, applauding.

Here the problems of characterising the speaker's feelings and of getting the right tone to characterise the conclusion of the performance give him trouble: he tries out many phrases for the finale of the music — "boiling to" — "floating like a liquid shout", "the shrilling ending shout". None of these remained in the printed version, which, for these two and a half lines, was evidently arrived at after the poem was transferred to the typewriter. Although Larkin, for once, had his last line in place before the poem begins, he still, characteristically, experiences difficulty making the transition to that final line, even after he has the pattern for his linking phrase in "And leaves me trying to pick out".

Once again, in this tender poem of immediate personal involvement we encounter a feature noted in the drafting of "Wild Oats" — lines worked over intensively that came in the first writing almost as they are in the printed version. The original phrasing, "One of your gloves unnoticed on the floor/Lies by your new, slightly outmoded shoes", differed from the final version of the lines only in the substitution of "Beside" for "Lies by"; yet the second line was subject to much redrafting. Indeed, in this eighteen-line poem, seven of the lines were first written down as (or almost as) they appear in the printed version; yet the drafting occupies four pages. The conclusion to be drawn is not that Larkin could not leave a good thing alone, but that he displays his mastery in being able to envisage and try out so many possibilities.

The interest of the drafting of these shorter poems is not confined to the rather obvious fact that some short poems came quickly and others took a long time. In the case of some of the satirical poems, such as "Breadfruit" or "Naturally the Foundation Will Bear Your Expenses", an embryo structure of comic rhymes importantly influences the structure of the poem in a way that seems not to have been the case with Larkin's longer poems. In a poem like "Broadcast", on the other hand, the leading concern is with finding phrases that will be true to and evocative of the feelings involved, and then fitting them to the rhyme scheme.

Chapter 11

POEMS PASSED OVER

When Larkin brought together *The Whitsun Weddings* in 1964, he included a number of poems that were written before *The Less Deceived* was sent to press in 1955. These were "Days", "Water", "Take One Home for the Kiddies" and "For Sidney Bechet". In addition, he included "Love Songs in Age", worked on at great length before the appearance of *The Less Deceived*, but not completed until 1957.

One reason for his not including the first three of these poems in *The Less Deceived* may have been that they were not in keeping with the ironic tone of the poems such as "Reasons for Attendance" or "Toads" that had been hailed as part of the new "Movement" before the appearance of *The Less Deceived*. Indeed, when "Days" was included in *The Whitsun Weddings*, it must have looked, to some readers, like a companion to "Nothing To Be Said", written in 1961. That poem certainly appears to constitute a return to the manner of "Days", indicating that Larkin had by then come to value the unambiguous lyricism of the earlier poem. Of course, it could be that he merely extracted these poems from his Workbooks when he was asked for poems for periodical publication during fallow periods when he had nothing to offer: "Water" and "Days" were published together in 1957, a year in which Larkin completed only one poem, the revived "Love Songs in Age". A further possibility is that "Water", "Days" and "Take One Home for the Kiddies" were originally passed over, along with the never-collected "Tops", because they came so easily and so casually.

Water

If I were called in
To construct a religion
I should make use of water.

Going to church
Would entail a fording
To dry, different clothes;

The entire drafting of "Water", Days" and "Take One Home for the Kiddies" is given, but not that of "For Sidney Bechet".

My litany would employ
Images of sousing,
A furious devout drench,

And I should raise in the east
A glass of water
Where any-angled light
Would congregate endlessly.

"Water" was drafted in a page and a half in April 1954.

                    were called in
If I ~~had been consulted~~
        To construct
~~On the making of~~ a religion
            make use of
I should ~~employ much~~ water

                    / to enter a
~~For instance, the way to church~~
~~Would lie~~ be

If I were called in
To ~~help~~ construct a religion
                more
I should make / use of water.

~~Go~~ To go
    ~~To go~~ to church   ~~a soaking~~
            entail a kind of ─?─?─?
    Would ~~mean~~ / fording
To ~~With~~ dry, different clothes. ~~after.~~

My litanies would employ
    ~~Words~~   ~~melting~~ drenching,
Images ~~Images~~ of ~~naked~~ water,
                unguarded
A   Furious ─?─ wet~~ness~~.
                ~~over above~~
~~High above~~ / ~~my~~
~~And on my altar~~
        And in the east window
A glass of water
        Would admit   from every direction
~~Through which all~~ light endlessly
~~Would pass and repass endlessly~~

                                6/4/54

On the previous page, on which he had completed the drafting of "Skin" the day before, there is a further sketch of the conclusion of "Water":

> My litanies would employ
> Images of sousing
> ~~unguarded unguarded~~
> A ~~furious vertical division~~.
>
> And I should raise in the east
> A glass of water
> ~~By~~
> ~~Through which all light~~ Through / which light ~~passes~~
> Should be Passes
> ~~? ? unhindered forever.~~ ~~Unhindered~~ from all sides.

As this passage seems closest to the printed version, it may be assumed that Larkin wrote these lines on the largely empty previous page after he had completed the first drafting.

The ease with which he arrived at the poem is characteristic of most of his few poems in free verse. Many of the changes are of choice of word or phrase: "called in" for "consulted"; "soaking", "melting", "drenching", "sousing". Once again, this illustrates Larkin's relationship with the complex forms that he used in his more ambitious poems. As one surveys the drafting of poems such as "The Whitsun Weddings", one does not have the sense that the demands of rhyme served to suggest the direction of the poems, but rather that Larkin exercised his ingenuity to accommodate an already sensed direction to the form. It is the demands of the form that give rise to much of the intense working of the longer poems.

Of some interest here is a piece of drafting that immediately follows "Reasons for Attendance" in Workbook No. 3, the Workbook in which "Water" is drafted:

> ~~You stand quite still~~
>
> ~~Clear still shape~~
>
> ~~Clear shaped stillness~~
>
> ~~Still, shaped clearness~~
>
> ~~Clear shape, admitting light~~
> ~~From every angle quarter point~~
> ~~Have even so your aisles~~

```
                admitting
        Still      allowing
        Clear shape admitting light
    Through one clear    sides    skin
        To your -?-  aisles
                all          around
        From every points of space  nameable
    By   clock or compass
        Compass or clock,
```

```
        stilled
        stilled
Filled  still shape, admitting light
        Through one clear skin
        From all points nameable
        By clock or by compass,
```

Beside the drafting is sketch of a glass of water, with the words "Fraught shape" under it. There seems here to have been a groping at the possibilities afforded by that image, which is later revived effectively in "Water". As is the case with "Water", the drafting sits among work that is in quite a different key.

"Days" seems to have developed rather casually, though it is one of Larkin's more memorable poems.

Days

What are days for?
Days are where we live.
They come, they wake us
Time and time over.
They are to be happy in:
Where can we live but days?

Ah, solving that question
Brings the priest and the doctor
In their long coats
Running over the fields.

In the midst of drafting "Next Please", Larkin wrote the lines

```
        look forward to
    Days we know will be happy
    Shine in the natural future
    White cairns of expectancy
```

He then moved to the next page, and proceeded to work them up into a poem, to which he gave the title "Tenth Days":

Days we anticipate
Shine in the natural future
We have only to wait
For the story-book happiness
                  counting
Whether as children ~~longing~~
The nights till

Days we anticipate
Shine in the natural future
And we need only
~~We have only to~~ wait
For their story-book happiness.
          night
Fireworks-~~night~~ for the child
  Fair day
~~The day trip~~ for the lovers —
     we are instantly
And ~~we are everything is~~ reconciled
     sad, slavish
To the ~~slavery and~~ mess
Of the other nine days
O bundle them aside!

Days we anticipate
Shine in the natural future,
And if we can but wait
Drop anchor in our lives

He took this no further, and returned to "Next Please". The first four lines of this uncompleted draft have very much the same movement as the opening lines of "Days".

In the spring of 1951, he wrote what is clearly the predecessor of "Days" — and also the descendent of "Tenth Days". There is just one page of drafting.

What are days for?
Days are to wake in
To discover our dear loves
Over and over
They are to be happy in
There is nowhere to live but days.

Why do nights come?
                hide
Nights are to ~~stay~~ in
When we have no loves
Or they have gone over
When ~~we~~ days have sickened us
Nights are to pretend in.

He returned to the poem after more than two years, apparently on August 3rd 1953. Again, the drafting occupies just one page.

What are days for?
Days are where we live.
    ~~Are~~ to be
Are ~~And~~   Are ? ? happy in
Over and over:
        ~~once we have woken up~~   When once they wake us
    ~~There is nowhere to live but days~~   ~~Let us once wake up~~
    ~~Days are all we have~~.   ~~There~~ is
                                ~~We can have nowhere else~~.

    And so
    ~~Why do~~ nights come⸍

What are days for?
Days are where we live,
And to be happy in
Over and over.
                a They come, they wake us
~~When~~   ~~Once they / wake us~~
Where ~~have we to live~~
       ~~We have nowhere to live~~ but days?
        can we live

_____

            ~~the~~
~~And so / nights come~~

What are days for?
Days are where we live
They come, they wake us,
  Time and time
~~Over and~~ over.
They are to be happy in:
Where can we live but days?

```
              to seek where
     And  seeking      they join
     Brings the priest and doctor
     On their long coats  running over the fields.
                              ?3 August 1953
```

The somewhat trite "day"/"night" comparison has been abandoned; and the poem is close to being the poem we know. Indeed, the triteness of much that was there originally has been removed to give a poem of deeply moving simplicity and directness.

As can be seen, the poem emerged quite unexpectedly; and, when returned to, revealed itself with very little drafting from Larkin. His reasons for coming back to it after long breaks are not clear. The situation seems quite the reverse of that in which he returned to some of his poems, such as "Love Songs in Age", that he had abandoned because he could not see how to complete them. Each time he worked on the poem that was to become "Days", it had the appearance of being almost completed — at least, for the time being. Instead of groping for the poem, as in parts of the drafting of "Church Going", Larkin would appear to have been taken by surprise.

Although the poem was completed in 1953, it was not published until it appeared in *Listen* for Summer-Autumn 1957 along with "Water". It was collected in *The Whitsun Weddings* in 1964.

"Take One Home for the Kiddies" was also put down and picked up again over a long period before completion.

Take One Home for the Kiddies

On shallow straw, in shadeless glass,
Huddled by empty bowls, they sleep:
No dark, no dam, no earth, no grass —
Mam, get us one of them to keep.

Living toys are something novel,
But it soon wears off somehow.
Fetch the shoebox, fetch the shovel —
Mam, we're playing funerals now.

The poem first emerged in April 1954, immediately after the drafting of "Water":

```
     "mam, it thinks that one's its mother!"
              stare through
        Faces  peering into  pet-shop glass,
At litters     hiding in each
```

? ? ?   / one another
-?- As they would have hid in grass

~~A short bewildering naked life~~

Naked, bewildering and short
"Mam, we're playin' funerals now."

"Mam, it thinks that one's its mother!"
Faces stare through pet-shop glass
At litters hiding in each other
As they would have hid in grass.

Living toys are novelties:
But novelty wears off, somehow,
        And
~~And now~~ they're so difficult to please

            s
Little toys, your novelty
        life will
Of ~~living~~ soon wears off, somehow.
    What matter
~~It's all right~~ if the kids are happy?
"Mam, we're playin' funerals now!"

        Pets

"Mam, it thinks that one's its mother!"
Faces stare through pet-shop glass
At litters hiding in each other
As they would have hid in grass.

Unique
~~Little~~ toys, your novelty
        living
Of ~~life will~~ soon wears off, somehow.
    ~~Still~~ you keep the children
But ~~What matter, if the kids~~ are happy:?
"Mam, we're playin' funerals now!"

                        18.4.54

The dating indicates a completed poem; though it was not used in
The Less Deceived. Larkin may have felt that it was a rather slight
poem. However, it was returned to in August 1960.

a Pet
Take a̶ ̶P̶e̶t̶ Home / for the Kiddies

L̶i̶f̶e̶ ̶i̶n̶ ̶t̶o̶y̶s̶ ̶a̶l̶i̶v̶e̶ ̶a̶r̶e̶
L̶i̶v̶i̶n̶g̶ ̶t̶o̶y̶s̶ are something s̶o̶m̶e̶t̶h̶i̶n̶g̶
Living toys are
L̶i̶f̶e̶ ̶i̶n̶ ̶l̶i̶t̶t̶l̶e̶ ̶t̶o̶y̶s̶ ̶i̶s̶ / novel
But it soon wears off, somehow/.
Fetch the shoebox, find the shovel —
"Mam, we're playing funerals now."

—

On shallow straw, in shadeless glass,
Huddled   By empty bowls, they sleep:
                    earth
No dark, no dawn, no r̶u̶n̶, no grass.
        get
"Mam, b̶u̶y̶ us one of them to keep."
                            13.8.60

The entire first stanza has been reworked, so that the concluding
lines of the two stanzas echo one another ironically. The fact that the
first stanza comes after the second in the redrafting was presumably
because Larkin was happy with his second stanza — and particularly
its striking final line. The poem did not appear in print for another
three years — until December 5th 1963, when it was published in the
Listener. There seems no special reason for the return to it in 1960.
It was collected in *The Whitsun Weddings* in 1964.
   "For Sidney Bechet", like "Days", had an interesting history.

For Sidney Bechet

That note you hold, narrowing and rising, shakes
Like New Orleans reflected on the water,
And in all ears appropriate falsehood wakes,

Building for some a legendary Quarter
Of balconies, flower-baskets and quadrilles,
Everyone making love and going shares —

Oh, play that thing! Mute glorious Storyvilles
Others may license, grouping round their chairs
Sporting-house girls like circus tigers (priced

Far above rubies) to pretend their fads,
While scholars *manqués* nod around unnoticed
Wrapped up in personnels like old plaids.

> On me your voice falls as they say love should,
> Like an enormous yes. My Crescent City
> Is where your speech alone is understood,
>
> And greeted as the natural noise of good,
> Scattering long-haired grief and scored pity.

The poem was started in December, 1953. Larkin drafted five lines, but did not return to it until he had written "Reasons for Attendance" and "I Remember, I Remember". He then drafted it to apparent completion and dated it "15.1.54" (in time for inclusion in *The Less Deceived*); though this dated draft lacks any attempt at the last two lines of the version as printed. However, on the page following this "completed" version, Larkin made what was evidently a fair copy of the poem. This copy additionally lacks the following last lines of the dated version on the previous page:

> ~~does~~
> On me your voice falls as they say love ~~should~~ should/,
> But doesn't   an unknown
> Seeming the exposition of ~~a~~ good
> That I contain, by which I am understood.

These lines are encountered in an abandoned poem from the next month, of which "On me your voice falls, as they say love should,/Like an immense agreement" is the opening. Larkin may well have gone back to the dated version of "Sidney Bechet" to rework it after the noted date and added these lines, which do not appear in the fair copy. The poem was still not as we know it, and was evidently completed in typescript. The poem first appeared in *Ark* in November, 1956. It was revived for publication in the more widely read *Listen* for Autumn 1962, evidently indicating its return to favour. It was included in *The Whitsun Weddings* two years later.

The history of these poems reflects a change of attitude on Larkin's part to his work after the publication of *The Less Deceived*. However, these poems arrived much more casually than did most of Larkin's poems; and the way in which they were returned to may indicate that Larkin did not recognise how good they were, just because they came so easily and unexpectedly.

Chapter 12

LARKIN'S MODE OF COMPOSITION

The workbooks give a very detailed picture of Larkin's mode of composition; but Larkin himself said very little about the process of writing poetry. Perhaps this was understandable, as he contended that it was "fatal to decide, intellectually, what good poetry is because you are then in honour bound to try to write it, instead of the poems that only you can write."[1] Indeed, while his style is unmistakable, he did not always seem to regard the attainment of an individual style as an end in itself. Introducing "The Explosion", he remarked, "What I should like to write is different kinds of poem that might be by different people."[2] For him the poet's business was "externalising and eternalising his own perceptions in unique and original verbal form."[3]

Some of his remarks were notorious for the way in which they seemed to scale down the pretensions of poetry. One of these occurred in the *Poetry Book Society Bulletin* that accompanied the publication of *The Whitsun Weddings* in 1964:

> To write a poem is a pleasure: sometimes I deliberately let it compete in the open market, so to speak, with other spare-time activities, ostensibly on the grounds that if a poem isn't more entertaining to write than listening to records or going out it won't be entertaining to read.[4]

Less aggressively, he explained elsewhere:

> . . . it was in the evening, after work, after washing up . . . It was a routine like any other. And really it worked very well. I don't think that you can write a poem for more than two hours.[5]

The consciously deflative tone is again unmistakable; though it is hard to see when else he might have written his poems, unless he had left the washing up until later. Indeed, the description fits the evidence of the workbooks very well. In later life, Larkin seems to have begun a new page of his workbook each time he sat down to write, and to have dated that page. We can see him coming back to poems evening after evening, and sometimes with a considerable gap between sessions, possibly reflecting his readiness for work on the poem, or possibly reflecting other commitments, which in those days could have been many.

All this points to a very deliberate approach to the writing of poetry. It is true, as Larkin said,

> A poem can come quickly. You just write it all out and then the next evening you alter a word or two and it's done. Another time it will take longer, perhaps months. What is always true is that the idea for a poem and a bit of it, a snatch or a line — it needn't be the opening line — come simultaneously. In my experience one never sits down and says I will now write a poem about this or that in the abstract.[6]

However, once embarked on a poem, Larkin generally stuck with it — though there were exceptions. Some of these have been described. He turned aside from "The Building" because he had promised "Going, Going" for a government publication. After beginning "The Whitsun Weddings", he stopped to write "Letter to a Friend about Girls". A few poems, such as "Take One Home for the Kiddies", he took up and put down in a desultory manner. The draftings of "MCMXIV" and "Talking in Bed" are interlaced with one another and are interrupted by the drafting of other poems. Nonetheless, his practice was to come back steadily to a poem before going on to another, working through it from beginning to end, stanza by stanza. As he accurately explained:

> I write — or used to — in notebooks in pencil, trying to complete each stanza before going on to the next. Then when the poem is finished I type it out, and sometimes make small alterations.[7]

The process could take months — even more than a year.

The process revealed in the composition of the longer poems discussed in this book — "Church Going", "The Whitsun Weddings", "Dockery and Son", "The Old Fools" and "The Building" — was remarkably uniform and in keeping with Larkin's description. He would begin with a line that was generally his first line, and this would often come at once in its final form. It would seem to have set the tone and movement of the poem, the remainder of which may have been rather nebulous. He would then assemble phrases or lines that were to be a part of his first stanza. These would be worked on until they gave him that first stanza. In the course of this work, the rhyme scheme would emerge. Sometimes the rhyme scheme would be set out independently. Once Larkin had his rhyme scheme and metrical form, he stayed with it. This was even true of "The Old Fools", where Larkin, uncharacteristically, jettisoned his first stanza, but nonetheless stayed with the stanza pattern he had evolved. In the case of "The Building", he drafted what appeared to be two-and-a-half stanzas before he hit on his very taxing pattern of a rhyme scheme that completed itself in eight lines with a stanza of seven lines. He then started over again, building his material into the pattern decided upon.

Larkin composed almost without exception, stanza by stanza, as he said. This may seem unsurprising at first: most poets begin at the beginning and follow the pattern of thought, narrative and syntax through to the conclusion, even though they may subscribe to the belief that every element in a poem reacts with every other, backwards or forwards. Some jump ahead; though few begin in the middle. A major exception was Dylan Thomas, whose later poems were often structured initially about words that he sought to have in particular places in his poems, creating an orchestration of words. T.S. Eliot attested that a poem might often begin as a rhythm about which a phrase coagulated. Most poets, it would seem, will go back over their poems, allowing later developments to bring about change in earlier passages. This was largely not true for Larkin; who, as he said, brought the drafting of each stanza to completion before going on to the next. From an examination of the way in which changes follow each other in the workbooks, it seems clear that he seldom went back over what he had done.

One reservation to this must be made concerning his frequent habit of writing out what he had done of a poem in fair copy before proceeding further. This would often be done when he was stuck as to how to proceed, or when he came back to a poem after a break. On such occasions, he might make changes throughout the fair copy as he wrote it out. Some of these changes would reflect his inveterate habit of changing his mind over and over concerning a word or phrase, often to arrive eventually at what was first written. In addition, of course, he made changes when the poems were transferred to typescript.

The traditional formal elements were important to Larkin: "metre and rhyme . . . I doubt really if I could operate without them";[8] and he seems to have relished difficult stanza patterns largely for the challenge they bring, as in "The Building". It should, of course, be remarked that metre and rhyme do not exhaust the traditional formal elements of poetry. Larkin's poetry has a strong narrative or discursive structure; but there is very little conscious attempt to exploit repeated or parallel phrases or images as structural devices. He also deliberately rejected structures of myth and intertextuality; and he strongly opposed obscurity and the concomitant use of discontinuities. His poetry depended heavily on the manipulation of tone; and he said that "Writing poetry is playing off the natural rhythms and word-order of speech against the artificialities of rhyme and metre"[9] — a remark that echoes what Robert Frost said in "The

Figure a Poem Makes".[10] It has already been noted that, as Larkin's stanzas evolve, the thought and narrative line lead the writing, and details and phrases are sometimes developed without regard for the rhyme scheme, only to be fitted in later. This is in keeping with a remark he made in a letter to Barbara Pym: "I am quite unable to do anything in the evenings — the notion of expressing sentiments in short lines having similar sounds at the ends seems as remote as mangoes on the moon."[11] There is a recognition here of the artificiality of poetry, and that composition presents itself to the poet as a series of problems. This contrasts with the procedures of some poets who employ traditional forms, and who allow the rhyme scheme to suggest the phrasing. Indeed, the music of the poem — its movement — does not seem to be what carries Larkin forward. Rather, much of the most intense drafting of Larkin's poetry results from his juggling with material until it not only fits his rhyme scheme, but gives him the movement and the tone that he wants, so that the drafting is sometimes like solving a puzzle. The drafting most resembles solving a puzzle in the composition of the satirical poems, particularly ones that came easily, like "Self's the Man". In some comic poems, of course, the rhymes themselves are among the most comic features; while the process of composition is not one of being true to a previously inarticulate sense of things, but one of exploiting the verbal structure for maximum effect, as is seen in the drafting of "Naturally the Foundation will Bear Your Expenses". There was no question, on the whole, of being true to something that actually happened, as was presumably the case in poems like "Broadcast".

The drafting seems least to resemble solving a puzzle in the case of Larkin's few poems in non-rhyming verse, as with "Going", "Water", "Days", or "Dublinesque". Here the phrases often came very easily; and the beauty of movement was not the result of extensive drafting. Indeed, we do not often see Larkin struggling — or even correcting himself — to get a musically acceptable phrase, as he does in "Dockery and Son", where he gets rid of the awkward repetition of "w" in the phrase "we without". In this respect, a good poet is like a good musician: we do not see him counting the beats in order to keep time. Larkin's ear was, from the beginning, extraordinarily good; and it is only in one or two places in the Workbooks that he makes any notation of scansion. One has the feeling that he did not write down a phrase unless it sounded right. His inveterate dickering was a matter of tuning things up.

The conception of writing conveyed by his practice and by his remarks is that of a process consciously controlled, while the function of rhetorical devices is seen as instrumental to the process rather than of its essence. We see in all this corroboration of the importance of subject, narrative, conscious thought, declarative statement and particular detail in Larkin's work. The stance of the poet, in his mature poems, is invariably that of someone making observations about a scene or event, arguing, drawing conclusions. The actual is present in its own right in his poetry, and not as a surrogate for something else. His poems seek to evoke the everyday world and to make statements about it. They are not oblique. The forms are traditional, and do not have an overall subordinating power, as, for example, in T.S. Eliot's *Four Quartets*. Larkin's remark concerning "The Whitsun Weddings" that "it only needed writing down"[12] may seem aggressively simplistic, but it reflects an attitude that was at the root of a great deal in his poetry: his notion that poetry was not merely the preservation of an experience, but that it should begin with something that actually happened and be true to what did happen. This was very far from the conception of poetry adopted by many other poets, and very notably far from Yeats's conception of poetry. Yet a poem should not be regarded as a complex or refined attempt to communicate something, but as a construct whose total effect is the *raison d'etre* of the poem. In this respect, theme or subject is not necessarily basic to a poem but may be regarded as just one more rhetorical choice open to the poet. As Robert Lowell remarked:

> Meaning varies in importance from poem to poem, and from style to style, but always it is only a strand and an element in the brute flow of composition . . . the author is an opportunist, throwing whatever comes to hand into his feeling for start, continuity, contrast, climax, and completion.[13]

While Larkin emphasised the importance for him of beginning with an experience and being true to an experience, he recognised that some experiences do not lead to poems and others do — an implied recognition that, in the perspective of successful composition, subject is a rhetorical choice. As he said, "I seem to have spent my life waiting for poems to turn up."[14] There is nothing particularly unusual in admitting to the vagaries of inspiration. However, in 1964, at the height of his powers, he gave a very acute discussion of those elements of creation that lie outside the artist's control:

> If something must be said, it should be about the poems one writes not necessarily being the poems one wants to write. Some years ago I came to the conclusion that to write a poem was to construct a verbal

device that would preserve an experience indefinitely by reproducing it in whoever read the poem . . . In so far as it suggested that all one had to do was pick an experience and preserve it . . . it was much over-simplified . . . The longer one goes on . . . the more one feels that some subjects *are* more poetic than others, if only that poems about them get written whereas poems about other subjects don't . . . This means that most of the time one is engaged in doing, or trying to do, something of which the value is doubtful and the mode of operation unclear . . . The days when one could claim to be the priest of a mystery are gone . . . Yet writing a poem is still not an act of the will. The distinction between subjects is not an act of the will. Whatever makes a poem successful is not an act of the will. In consequence, the poems that actually get written may seem trivial or unedifying, compared with those that don't. But the poems that get written, even if they do not please the will, evidently please that mysterious something that has to be pleased . . . there must be among the ingredients that go towards the writing of a poem a streak of curious self-gratification, almost impossible to describe except in some such terms, the presence of which tends to nullify any satisfaction the will might be feeling at a finished job.[15]

The passage brings into focus the often discommoding role in creation of those elements of the self that lie beyond the reach of the will; and there is a recognition that the poet does not *elect* his themes or subjects, and cannot impose his own sense of what is important on what he writes. As Larkin put it elsewhere: "Very little that catches the imagination . . . can get its clearance from either the intelligence or the moral sense. And equally, properly truthful and dispassionate themes enlist only the wannest support from the imagination. The poet is perpetually in that common human condition of trying to feel a thing because he believes it, or believe a thing because he feels it."[16] He points to one of the most mysterious and paradoxical features of literature, for both writer and reader; and evidence of how true this was for him is to be found in the quite large number of poems in the workbooks, such as "The Dance", that he was unable to complete, despite extensive work on them.

These remarks are borne out by the drafting of poems that were completed. As Larkin commented:

I used to find that I was never sure I was going to finish a poem until I had thought of the last line. Of course, the last line was sometimes the first one you thought of! But usually the last line would come when I'd done about two-thirds of the poem, and then it was just a matter of closing the gap.[17]

When he had got his first line, Larkin did not have great difficulty in drafting his first stanza, which would frequently consist of physical details of the circumstance of the poem. Finding a way forward might present some difficulty; but, once this had been done, narrative details would often come very easily. It was at the point at which Larkin had to discover the way that the poem was to end — the point at which he had to make his poem move in that direction — that created the greatest difficulty and saw the most drafting, often with no immediately clear sense of direction. This might be described as the *peripeteia* of the poem — the turning-point at which it revealed itself to both author and reader.

This particular moment of the poem frequently had another revealing feature. Larkin, in attempting to evoke the key emotion at this point of resolution, would be drawn to developing metaphors that came from the general stock of poetry rather than from the setting of the poem. We see this strongly in "Deceptions", "Church Going", "The Whitsun Weddings" and "Dockery and Son". Invariably, these metaphors would be dropped and the passage would be developed in terms of realistic detail drawn from the setting of the poem — detail that often had a submerged metaphorical function, as with the "ranged/Joining and parting lines" of "Dockery and Son" or the "tightened brakes" in "The Whitsun Weddings". As is evident, Larkin sometimes chose to conclude his more ambitious poems with a metaphor that came from the general poetic stock — the "arrow-shower" in "The Whitsun Weddings", the "sand clouds" in "Dockery and Son", and the "alp" in "The Old Fools". Whether these metaphors are as telling as "Your hands, tiny in all that air applauding" in "Broadcast" or the "wasteful, weak, propitiatory flowers" in "The Building", taken from the scenes of the poems themselves, is a matter for debate. Undoubtedly the change of gear seemed to Larkin to constitute an important enhancement; and, in his recorded reading of "The Whitsun Weddings", he makes a decided change of tone when he comes to the final metaphor. When he encountered "a hunger in himself to be more serious", he was frequently tempted by the conventionally poetic; but this temptation was finally resisted, and the poems emerged with that firm sense of the particularity of everyday details that was his strength. It would be wrong here to speak of the continuing influence of Yeats; but it would be right to contend that there lurked for him a longing for the transcendant that Yeats had satisfied. The power of his poetry to some degree derives from the intensity of that longing, resisted with such firm realism in his best work. This conflict makes itself felt in the drafting.

As Larkin said, "Everyday things are lovely to me";[18] and his poetry is at its most telling when he is evoking such details in their pathetic ordinariness. Many of his poems are replete with such details, as in "Here", "The Big Store", "Ambulances" or "The Whitsun Weddings". In that last poem, he expends a great deal of drafting on the details of what is seen from the carriage window in the second stanza. Yet these details, so evocative of the English afternoon landscape and of the stillness that the speaker feels at this point, do not have a metaphoric function in the poem. Larkin's drafting was not aimed at this; and one can safely say that this was not a structural feature that he sought to develop at this point in the poem. The same may be said of the list of places in which the dis-used pre-marital name still lurks in "Maiden Name" — another list that Larkin drafted extensively. We see an exemplification of what has sometimes been called the "novelistic" tendency of Larkin's poetry; though the metaphorical use of detail is a feature of many novels, not least Larkin's *A Girl in Winter*. As Dan Jacobson reported, when he interviewed Larkin for *The New Review*, "He had to find a way of bringing into his poetry the interests and range of emotions which he had previously believed could be expressed only in novels . . . "[19] With this came a novelistic and frequently dramatised structure of narrative.

Larkin's poetry leans strongly towards the structures encountered in normal conversational use of speech. The dominant structures in his poetry, both for him and for his readers, are those of declarative statement and narrative. If we look for a submerged *structure* of metaphor or figurative use of realistic detail, we will seldom find one; and we do not expect to find structures of myth or intertexuality. It cannot be said, either, that we encounter poems that seem to be about something other than what they foreground; though several attempts have been made to see poems by Larkin as symptomatic of something other than what the writer appears to intend. His style depends strongly on communicative codes particular to the culture group to which he belonged; and there is little evidence of circumspection regarding these codes, either in the composition of the poems or in the completed poems. Apart from this, one can say of Larkin's poetry that the writer not only seems very much aware of what is going on in his poems, but that he favours a type of writing in which this is the case.

If anything is disarming in Larkin's mature work, it is the way in which very artful poetic constructs are made to appear so casual. The work in the drafting is expended considerably on tone and the manner of simulated speech, words being written out, crossed out

and written out again. Very frequently these are particles or con-
junctions: "the"/"this"/"a"/"some", or "and"/"but"/"so"/,"then",
represent the types of choice that Larkin would manoeuvre around,
presumably in an attempt to get the right tone and the right type of
continuity.

The workbooks show us the drafting. In keeping with Larkin's
belief in writing poems based on personal experience, not on material derived from literature, the origins of some of his poems can be
traced to events in his life, as recounted in Andrew Motion's biography or in Larkin's own recollections in interviews and articles. This
biographical information has been set out in the discussion of individual poems. The only accounts of the writing of some of his poems are
in the introductory remarks to his recorded reading of his work. He
seldom refers to his poems in letters written after his early twenties.

The workbooks offer only a few hints concerning the gestation of
the poems. These are the small number of notes that Larkin wrote to
himself. Some of these have been cited already. On two occasions he
wrote out plans for subjects for poems. The first was early in 1953:
"*Subjects for poems*:/Ballads/Waltzes/What everything has changed
to: the mechanism of this." This was followed a few pages later by
"*Waltzes*":

> Once the chance of hearing one of the old tunes was very small, unless
> an old fiddler came one's way, but now any radio shop or cinema or-
> gan or band on the pier may suddenly strike from nowhere, + all the
> constellated emotion come back. [Waltz Theme]

Nothing seems to have come of this, though the idea may have
borne fruit in "Love Songs in Age". The other note, from the end of
1953, is to write a set of poems about the seasons:

> *Spring — Summer — Autumn — Winter*
> Four poems or groups of poems. Dealing for the most part in natural
> descriptions, but each taking as central theme the commonest feature
> of its time—resurrection, luxuriance, decay, death—+ the whole to
> have the progress to death as a backbone. To be written, I suppose,
> at leisure, making notes on the seasons as they come up.

This follows, by a month or so, the composition of "Autumn" in
October. Another version of this note is dated "11/11/53" and is
headed "The Seasons". It concludes "the whole is to be a progress
to death, as our life is". It is followed by further work on "Autumn".
Nothing seems to have come of this idea, unless the incomplete "Summer Poem" of August, 1960, or "January" of June 1961, are related

to it. The plan does not suggest poetry of the kind in which Larkin excelled: "Autumn" is certainly not one of his characteristic or best remembered poems.

Larkin also wrote short passages about poetry in the beginning of his workbooks — admonitions in some cases.

> These poems are intended to be read silently with the eye. If by any chance any should be read aloud, the reader is asked to use a tone of voice similar to that in which he would carefully direct a stranger in the street.
>
> (Workbook 2, c. 1953)

> I try, whenever the poetic (as opposed to the sensational) presents itself, to describe what seemed to produce it, and in this way to reproduce it for others to experience it.
>
> (Workbook 3, c. 1954)

> A poem is a verbal device intended to preserve emotion indefinitely, and reproduce it/by reproducing it indefinitely.
>
> (Workbook 4, c. 1954)

> Never write anything because you think it is true, only because you think it is beautiful.
>
> (Workbook 7, c. 1972)

As can be seen, everything, except the first statement, is reflected in Larkin's published writings or interviews.

What have been discussed so far are features of Larkin's poetry that he must have been aware of or would easily have become aware of in examining his workbooks. Yet he himself acknowledged the element of mystery in the matter of which poems come to be successfully completed and which do not. The poem, at the commencement of composition, remains for many poets in some respects numinous, something to be realised in the process of composition. The work of imagination that comes between the events and the drafting is largely hidden from us; while the process of realisation is what we see taking place in a poet's workbooks. As Larkin said, "in some poems the work you have to do, the effort you have to put in, goes towards following up the original gift, the original few words, the original vision, and seeing where it leads, finding out its natural development".[20] It is interesting to ask what assumptions or unconscious processes lie hidden behind Larkin's seemingly direct and open style of composition — and to ask whether the workbooks reveal anything here.

The very "understandable" style of writing, with its clarity, directness and its maintenance of the normal conventions of speech and thought, suggests that experience can be understood and characterised with the clarity that the poems attain. Indeed, the adoption of such a style might imply a strong need on Larkin's part to find that this is the case. The pressure to keep aspiration in place, so disturbing to some earlier readers of Larkin's poetry, is to be associated with the obvious longing for transcendence that is almost always set aside. The evidence of these pressures in Larkin's proclivity for trying out conventional metaphors (later rejected) at crucial moments of composition has already been remarked upon.

Within the controlled and seemingly transparent style of poetry that Larkin attains, there are things going on that may not have been obvious to him or to his readers. Woven into some poems, there is a structure of conceded positions, accompanied at times by a pronounced steering of the reader to make the required concession. However, there may not have been an awareness of the structure of concession in all cases. In "The Whitsun Weddings", the "we" of the conclusion — Larkin and the married couples on the train — is not the implied "we" of the poem; and the implied "we" is not just anybody who happens to be reading the poem. It is clearly the cultural group from which Larkin came — a group that recognised that you don't wear a belt with a suit and that there is something less than glamorous about weddings celebrated in "bunting-dressed/Coach-party annexes". Indeed, the feeling of transformation that comes at the end of the poem depends on this social placing being shared without negative reflection by the reader. The details of social placing caused Larkin little trouble in the composition of the poem; and this would seem to indicate how unreflectively his stance was taken by Larkin.

In "Church Going" we have an extensive structure of assumed concession, as in "But what remains when disbelief has gone", which invites the assumption that eventually nobody will bother about religious belief one way or another, though the asumption is not openly made. There is much groping in the drafting of "Church Going", but not concerning this sentence. Similarly, the wonderfully contrived sentence

> Or will he be my representative,
>
> Bored, uninformed, knowing the ghostly silt
> Dispersed, yet tending to this cross of ground
> Through suburb scrub because it held unspilt
> So long and equably what since is found

> Only in separation — marriage, and birth,
> And death, and thoughts of these — for which was built
> This special shell?

makes a profound compliment to the Church, but does this in passing
in the middle of a question. It seems artfully to assume the reader's
agreement, without raising any question that might give rise to open
disagreement. Yet, when we examine the drafting, much of the sentence seems to have come quite easily; while the final form, in which
the initial question and its conclusion dominate the sentence, is not
encountered in the Workbook, and was evidently arrived at by Larkin
in transferring the lines to the typewriter.

Indeed, the parts of a composition that come most easily to a writer
can be as revealing as those over which he expends the most work;
and the features of Larkin's poetry just discussed have been criticised
by Andrew Crozier:

> we detect in the poet's authority a restless determination of poetic
> discourse and foreclosure of the intended audience. The discourse is
> emphatically singular in many cases, while 'we' . . . implies a restricted
> group.[21]

Crozier offers a contrasting characterisation of a different type of poetry — Apocalyptic poetry — which he sees as presenting

> a dense, often violent rhetoric, from which the guiding and control-
> ling presence of a speaker — constructing the poem's framework of
> interpretation around its personal authority, and furnishing its em-
> pirical experience as the horizon of the poem's range of reference — is
> excluded.[22]

Indeed, a writer may not be aware of many cultural aspects of his
speech and of the cultural resonances to which they give rise; but
such resonances are unavoidable and are inevitably felt most strongly
in a particular cultural group, however wide. The exploitation of
those resonances that are most natural and intimate is intrinsic to any
effective use of language; and for Larkin, finding his style was finding
poetry in a language that was the customary speech of thought and
feeling for him and for the culture group from which he came. We
see this style achieved rather suddenly in "Lines on A Young Lady's
Photograph Album".

Much of what contributes to a writer's performance he will be
aware of only peripherally, especially those aspects of his writing that
come with little effort. These will be the things in which his talent

manifests itself the most strongly; and these aspects of the writing will require the least effort in drafting — in contrast with the attempts that, as Larkin remarked, mysteriously come to nothing. The bent of the talent will manifest itself often in the features from which the writing takes its start: in an opening phrase with a particular tone and movement for Larkin; in an image for Yeats. It is, of course, those aspects of composition that require the most work that are seen in a writer's workbooks; and Larkin's workbooks are no exception.

Larkin's poetry is situated at one end of the spectrum of poetic composition. There is a conscious rejection of certain structural devices, such as myth and intertextuality; and a conscious espousal of features, such as clarity, that imply the development of normal continuities in structures such as syntax, logical argument or narrative. The imagery, on the whole, does not operate metaphorically; and structures of metaphor are seldom encountered. Nonetheless, the workbooks remain highly revealing examples of composition because of the sensitivity to the possibilities inherent in every feature of a poem that is exemplified in the very detailed drafting. We are given an insight into his mastery through his awareness of so much to be explored in differences that to the common eye might seem so small.

Yet, while the workbooks reveal a great deal about Larkin's mode of composition, they cannot and do not show us everything. The device of making the speaker of a poem a *persona* that is a comic version of himself and whose authority is deflated by an ironic conclusion seems to have come full-formed in one go in "Reasons for Attendance" (possibly on the example of Kingsley Amis's "Something Nasty in the Bookshop"). When Larkin was asked how he arrived at the image of the toad for work or labour, he replied "Sheer genius";[23] and we must accept that some inventive parts of composition will remain mysterious. So many aspects of talent *are* mysterious; and what one is talented in is not a matter of choice. The boy who can do wonderful imitations of the headmaster and who goes on to be a comedian does not chose his vocation because it seems to him the most worthy. The writer is in the same situation, caught between what he feels impelled to do and what he is capable of doing. Some things will come easily; others will not come at all, as Larkin recognised. In the workbooks we see him struggling with the obdurate and also writing brilliantly and with ease. Parts of the process must remain hidden. We must be grateful for what the workbooks enable us to see.

A NOTE ON THE SOURCES

Philip Larkin was actively concerned that the manuscripts of British writers should find their way into British libraries. He chaired the committee that was responsible for the Arts Council Collection of Modern Literary Manuscripts and wrote an introduction to its descriptive catalogue produced by Jenny Stratford. In demonstration of his concerns, he deposited his earliest workbook in the Arts Council Collection in the British Library. After his death, the remainder of his workbooks consitituted part of his estate; and, following the resolution of certain legal problems arising from his will, the workbooks were deposited in Hull at the Brynmor Jones Library, of which Larkin had been the head for many years.

The Workbook in the Arts Council Collection, BM Ad MS 52619, is described in *The Arts Council Collection of Modern Literary Manuscripts* by Jenny Stratford:

> Folio notebook, stiff black covers, and spine, *printed* label PHILIP LARKIN (f. i), 1944–1950. Old pagination, rectos only, pp. 1–121 (ff. 1–55). Pages torn out before and after pagination, and in the remainder of the notebook. Many stubs remain, those with fragments of writing being foliated. F. ii is a photograph of Yeats broadcasting; f. iii an untitled typescript copy of his 'The Collar-Bone of a Hare'. Miscellaneous notes and quotations are ff. iv, v.[1]

Stratford listed all the poems in the Workbook, with dates, dividing them into sections: *The North Ship*; *Twenty Poems*; Uncollected poems; and Unpublished poems. She identified those poems that had been included in the typescript of the then unpublished volume, *In the Grip of Light*.

The remaining Workbooks are described in *Manuscripts and other documents deposited by the Executors of the Larkin Estate*, compiled by Brian Dyson and issued by the Brynmor Jones Library, University of Hull.[2] The books are, in appearance, similar to the notebook in the Arts Council collection.

(The complete description of the Archives contains the following sections, not all reproduced here.

1–12   Poetry workbooks
13–17   Poetry typescripts
18–20   Poetry publications
21–29   Prose and other manuscripts
30–36   Correspondence
37–40   Interviews
41–43   Speeches
44–47   All Souls College, Oxford
48–52   Photographs
53–66   Miscellaneous

Some reference to items in these sections occurs in the description of the workbooks.)

The numbers in brackets on the left-hand side of the page are reference numbers earlier assigned by the Larkin Estate.

POETRY WORKBOOKS

(59) 1. Workbook No. 2 (25.7× 20.2cm). Contains drafts of poems (in pencil).
12 Mar. 1950–[Sept. ?] 1951

2. Items formerly inserted loosely in 1 above and removed for safe-keeping:

At page dated 19 May 1959: –

a. ALS. 'Jim' (Sutton) to PAL   (May 1950?)

At the rear: –

b. Part of page torn (from Workbook No. 1, British Museum Addl.MS MS 52619, p. 76)   13 May 1949

c. Page torn from a diary or record of dreams
26–29 Dec. (1942)

d. 'The march past'. Annotated. [CP55]   [25 May 1951]

e. 'To my wife'. [CP54]   [19 Mar. 1951]

f. 'Pigeons in Winter' (ms., with drafts). Later published as 'Pigeons'. [CP109]   27 Dec. 1955

g. 'Under a splendid chestnut tree'. Annotated. [CP43–44]
[June 1950]

h. 'Epigram on an academic marriage' (ms., being part of a page torn from Workbook No. 1)   19 May 1949

Verso: Early draft of part of 'Fiction and the Reading Public' (ms.). *See also* 28

i. 'For I.C.L.' First line: "The point of a stick, drawn" (m.s., being page torn from Workbook No. 1). *See also* 14(ae)
30 May 1946–3 June 1946

Verso: "There is no clearer speaking"   12 June 1946

j. "Her birthday always has Real rabbit weather" (Title: 'Tea out of doors'?). (m.s.)   n.d.

k. 'Long Last'. [CP151]. *See also* 8(m)   [3 Feb. 1963]

l. Likewise (carbon)

m. Queen's University of Belfast Film Society, *Film news*, v. 2, no. 5
                                                    14 Jan. 1953

n. 'Marriages'. Annotated. [CP63]   [12 June 1951]

(58)   3. Workbook No. 3 (25.7× 20.2cm)   24 Jan. 1953–26 May 1954

(61)   4. Workbook No. 4 (25.7×20.2cm)   10 June 1954–6 Sept. 1954

(56)   5. Workbook No. 5 (25.7× 20.2cm). The first 13 pages contain an auto-
       biographical essay (late 1940s?). The early pages of draft poems are
       dated Nov. 1953, 15 Jan. 1955 and then 19 Sept. 1956–7, Nov. 1960
                                                    Nov. 1953–Nov. 1960

       6. Inserted loosely at the rear of 5 above: –

       a. Press cuttings. (2)   n.d.

       b. Qutoations. (2)   1928; n.d.

       c. Blank sheet of notepaper, headed 'Sligachan Hotel, Isle of Skye'

       7. Workbook No. 6 (25.7× 20.2cm)   14 Jan. 1960–12 May 1964

       8. Inserted loosely at the front of 7 above: –

       a. 'Ignorance of Death' (3 lines of prose)   n.d.

       b. Cutting. 'Dockery and Son', from *The Listener*. [CP152]
                                                         11 Apr. 1963

       c. Cutting. 'Toads Revisited', from *The Spectator*. [CP147]
                                                         23 Nov. 1962

       d. Cutting. 'Send no Money', from *The Observer*. [CP146]
                                                         18 Nov. 1962

       e. Cutting. 'Here', from *The New Statesman*. [CP136]   24 Nov. 1961

       f. Cutting. 'As bad as a Mile', from *The Listener*. [CP125]
                                                         12 Dec. 1963

       g. Cutting. 'Take One Home for the Kiddies', from *The Listener*.
       [CP130]   5 Dec. 1963

       h. Cutting. 'Broadcast', from *The Listener?*. [CP140]   25 Jan. 1962

i. Cutting (from *The Listener*), including photograph of George Hartley   25 Nov. 1962

j. Cutting. 'Essential Beauty', from *The Spectator*. [CP144]
5 Oct. 1962

k. 'Love'. [CP150]. *See also* 12(f)   [7 Dec. 1962]

l. 'Holiday'. Annotated.   n.d.

m. 'Long Last'. [CP151]. *See also* 2(k), 2(l)   [3 Feb. 1963]

(60) 9. Workbook No. 7 (25.7× 20.2cm)   6 Oct. 1964–10 Jan. 1972

10. Inserted loosely in 9 above: –

At the front: –

a. Queen's University of Belfast. Men's Hostel (Queen's Chambers)
Bill for accommodation and laundry   30 June 1951

At page dated 12 Oct. 1971: –

b. Cutting. 'Livings', from *The Observer*. [CP186]   20 Feb. 1972

At the rear: –

c. 'When my diary ended'. Annotated. Ill.   Feb. 1967

d. Loose page containing list of girls' names. *Verso* ill.   (1966?)

e. Cutting. 'Friday Night in the Royal Station Hotel', from the (Sheffield) *Morning Telegraph*. Corrected by PAL. [CP163]   7 Jan.
1967

f. Cutting. 'The Trees', from the *New Statesman*. [CP163]. *See also*
10(n)   18 May 1968

g. 'Letter to a Friend about Girls'. Slight variant of CP122. *See also*
10(l), 10(ab), 12(b), 12(e), 16(f)   [Dec. 1959]

h. Cutting. 'Homage to a Government', from *The Sunday Times*.
[CP171]   19 Jan. 1969

i. 'Annus Mirabilis'. [CP167]. *See also* 10(s), 10(ab)   [16 June 1967]

j. Photocopied page proof. 'To the Sea', from the *London Magazine*.
Corrected by PAL. [CP173]   [Jan. 1970]

k. 'How high they build hospitals'. Annotated (later published as
'How' in *Wave*, Autumn 1970). [CP176]   [10 Apr. 1970]

l. 'Letter to a Friend about Girls'. Annotated. Slight variant. *See
also* 10(g), 10(ab), 12(b), 12(c), 16(f)   [Dec. 1959]

m. 'High Windows'. Annotated. [CP165]   [12 Feb. 1967]

n. Page proof. 'The Trees', from *The New Statesman*. [CP166]. *See
also* 10(f)   [18 May 1968]

o. 'Cut Grass'. [CP183]. *See also* 10(u)   [3 June 1971]

p. Page proof. 'Vers de Société', from *The New Statesman*. [CP181].
    See also 10(t)   [18 June 1971]

q. 'This be the Verse'. [CP180]   [Apr.? 1970]

r. 'Solar'. Annotated. [CP159]   [4 Nov. 1964]

s. 'Annus Mirabilis'. (Photocopy). [CP167]. *See also* 10(i), 10(ad)
                                                             [16 June 1967]

t. 'Vers de Société'. [CP181]. *See also* 10(p)   19 May 1971]

u. Cutting. 'Cut Grass', from *The Listener*. [CP183]. *See also* 10(o)
    29 July 1971

v. Cutting. 'How Distant', from *The Listener*. [CP162] 26 Oct. 1967

w. Cutting. 'Posterity' [CP170] and 'Sad Steps' [CP169] from *The New
    Statesman*   28 June 1968

x. 'The Explosion'. [CP175]   [5 Jan. 1965]

y. 'Laboratory Monkeys'. Alternative title in pencil 'Ape Experiment
    Room' (as it appears in CP160)   [Feb. 1965]

z. 'Clouds', 'Dwelling places', 'Light'. Annotated   n.d.

aa. 'Sympathy in White Major'. Annotated. [CP168]   [31 Aug. 1967]

ab. 'Letter to a Friend about Girls'. (Photocopied t.s.). *See also* 10(g),
    10(l), 12(b), 12(e), 16(f). [CP122]   [Dec. 1959]

ac. 'I have started to say'. Annotated. [CP185]   [Oct. 1971]

ad. 'Annus Mirabilis'. Annotated. [CP167]. *See also* 10(i), 10(s)
                                                             [16 June 1967]

ae. Notice. University of Hull Staff Sports Club Dance   10 May 1963

(54) 11. Workbook No. [8]. (32×20cm). Just over half used. The last entry,
          'Good for you, Gavin', is undated   11 Jan. 1972–20 Nov. 1980

12. Inserted loosely in 11 above.

At the front: –

a. 'The Mower'. [CP214]. *See also* 12(d), 12(m)   [12 June 1979]

b. 'Letter to a friend about girls'. Annotated. Sent to Anthony
    Thwaite and signed 'Horatio Larkin'. (Photocopy). [CP122]. *See
    also* 10(g), 10(l), 10(ab), 12(e), 16(f)   [Dec. 1959]

c. 'Heads in the Women's Ward'. Annotated. [CP194] [6 Mar. 1972]

d. Photocpy of 12(a) above

e. 'Letter to a Friend about Girls'. Variant. No annotation. (Photo-
    copy). [CP122]. *See also* 10(g), 10(l), 10(ab), 12(b), 16(f)
                                                             [Dec. 1959]

f. 'Love'. Variant. Annotated. [CP150]. *See also* 8(k)   [7 Dec. 1962]

g. Cutting. 'The Old Fools', from *The Listener*. [CP196]. *See also* 12(h)   [1 Feb. 1973]

h. Photocopy. Proof copy of 'The Old Fools', corrected by PAL. [CP196]. *See also* 12(g)   25 Jan. 1973

i. 'Femmes Damnées'. [CP270]   1943
   Verso: Photocopied t.s. of 'Examitis', by Duncan Forbes

j. 'Good for you, Gavin'. (Photocopied ms.). [CP216] [26 Nov. 1981]

k. 'The View'. Annotated (title altered from 'The View from Fifty'). [CP195]   [Aug.? 1972]

At the rear: –

l. 'Love Again'. Variant. [CP215]   20 Sept. 1979

m. 'The Mower'. (Photocopy). [CP214]. *See also* 12(a), 12(d)
                                                                    [12 June 1979]

n. 'When first we faced, and touching showed'. [CP205]
                                                                    [20 Dec. 1975]

o. 'Morning at last: there in the snow'. Annotated. [CP206]
                                                                    [1 Feb. 1976]

p. 'The Winter Palace'. Annotated. [CP211]   [1 Nov. 1978]

q. 'Long lion days'. Annotated. (ms.). [CP219]   21 July 1982

r. 'The little lives of earth and form'. (ms.). [CP207]   8 May 1977

REFERENCES

CHAPTER 1

1. Rilke, R.M. — *Sonnette an Orpheus/Sonnets to Orpheus*, trans. M.D. Herter (New York: Norton, 1962), 2,2.
2. "Operation Manuscript", *Poetry in the Making*, ed. Jenny Lewis (London: Turret Books, 1967).
3. "Writing Poems", *Required Writing* (London: Faber, 1983) 83.
4. "An Interview with *Paris Review*", *Required Writing*, 70.

CHAPTER 2

1. "Introduction to *The North Ship*", *Required Writing*, 29.
2. "Introduction to *The North Ship*", *Required Writing*, 28–29.
3. Stratford, Jenny — *The Arts Council Collection of Modern Literary Manuscripts* (London: Turret Books, 1974).
4. Letter to A.T. Tolley, Sept. 30, 1982.
5. "Introduction to *The North Ship*", *Required Writing*, 30.

CHAPTER 3

1. "Poet on the 8.15" — Interview with Philip Larkin, by John Horder, *The Guardian* (May 20, 1965) 9.
2. "The Poetry of Hardy", *Required Writing*, 175.
3. Jacobson, D. — "Philip Larkin — a profile", *The New Review* I,3 (June 1974) 27.
4. Motion, Andrew — *Philip Larkin* (London: Methuen, 1982) 35.
5. Letter to A.T. Tolley, Sept. 30, 1982.
6. "Monitor", BBC TV1, Dec. 15, 1964.
7. Letter to A.T. Tolley, Sept. 30, 1982.

CHAPTER 4

1. Hartley, A. — "Critic Between the Lines", *The Spectator* (Jan. 8, 1954) 47.
2. Hartley, A. — "Poets of the Fifties," *The Spectator* (Aug. 27, 1954) 261.
3. "An Interview with *Paris Review*", *Required Writing*, 74.
4. Regan, Stephen — *Philip Larkin* (London: Macmillan, 1992) 107–8.
5. Hartley, Jean — *Philip Larkin, the Marvell Press and Me* (Manchester: Carcanet, 1989) 82.

CHAPTER 5

1. "The Pleasure Principle", *Required Writing*, 80–82.
2. Russell, Bertrand — *Introduction to Mathematical Philosophy*, Ch. 16. "Descriptions" (London: Allen & Unwin, 1919).
3. Haffenden, 90.

CHAPTER 6

1. Haffenden, John — "The True and the Beautiful: a conversation with Philip Larkin" *London Magazine* 20, 1 & 2 (April/May 1980) 91.
2. *Selected Letters* (London: Faber, 1992) 227.

CHAPTER 7

1. "An Interview with *Paris Review*", *Required Writing*, 75.
2. Haffenden, 92.
3. Recounted by Professor John White, University of Hull.
4. Hartley, 119.
4. Larkin Archive MS 15(d) and MS16(b).
6. "An Interview with *Paris Review*", *Required Writing*, 74.
7. *Philip Larkin reads and comments on* The Whitsun Weddings (Listen LPV 6 — Hessle: The Marvell Press, c. 1965).
8. Motion, 288.
9. Haffenden, 92.
10. *Philip Larkin reads and comments on* The Whitsun Weddings.

CHAPTER 8

1. Motion, 333.
2. "The Traffic in the Distance", *Required Writing*, 277; and Scrimingeour, P.D. "Philip Larkin's 'Dockery and Son' and Julian Hall's *The Senior Commoner*" *Notes & Queries* (June 1986) 33 (231) (2) 193.
3. Woolf, Virginia — *To The Lighthouse* (New York: Harcourt, Brace, 1927) 154.
4. Haffenden, 84.
5. "Not Like Larkin", *The Listener* (Aug. 17, 1972) 209.

CHAPTER 9

1. Motion, 418.

CHAPTER 10

1. Haffenden, 96.
2. "An Interview with *Paris Review*", *Required Writing*, 58.
3. *Philip Larkin reads and comments on* The Whitsun Weddings.
4. Motion, 320.
5. "An Interview with *Paris Review*", *Required Writing*, 58.

CHAPTER 12

1. "Statement", *Required Writing*, 79.
2. "Not Like Larkin", 209.
3. "Subsidising Poetry", *Required Writing*, 89.
4. "Writing Poems", *Required Writing*, 84.
5. "An Interview with *Paris Review*", *Required Writing*, 58.
6. "An Interview with the *Observer*", *Required Writing*, 52.
7. "An Interview with *Paris Review*", *Required Writing*, 70.
8. "Four Conversations", Ian Hamilton, *London Magazine* n.s. 4, 8 (November 1964) 73.
9. "An Interview with *Paris Review*", *Required Writing*, 71.
10. Frost, Robert — "The Figure a Poem Makes", *Selected Prose of Robert Frost*, ed. H. Cox and E.C. Lathem (New York: Holt, Rinehart and Winston, 1966) 18.
11. *Selected Letters*, 521.
12. Haffenden, 92.
13. Lowell, Robert — "On Skunk Hour" *Collected Prose* (New York: Farrar, Strauss, Giroux, 1987) 225.
14. "Not Like Larkin", 209.
15. "Writing Poems", *Required Writing*, 83–84.
16. Contribution to "Poetry 1962: context", *London Magazine* n.s. 1, 11 (Feb. 1962) 32.
17. "An Interview with *Paris Review*", *Required Writing*, 58.
18. Haffenden, 92.
19. Jacobson, Dan — "Philip Larkin: A Profile", *The New Review* 1, 3 (June 1974) 27.
20. *Philip Larkin reads and comments on* The Whitsun Weddings.
21. Crozier, Andrew — "Thrills and Frills" in *Society and Literature: 1945–1970*, ed. A. Sinfield (London: Methuen, 1983) 205.
22. Crozier, 228.
23. "An Interview with *Paris Review*", *Required Writing*, 74.

A NOTE ON SOURCES

1. Stratford, Jenny — *The Arts Council Collection of Modern Literary Manuscripts*.
2. *Manuscripts and other documents deposited by the Executors of the Larkin Estate* (Hull: Brynmor Jones Library, 1991; rev. ed. 1994).

INDEX OF POEMS DISCUSSED

Larkin at Work

This publication was produced using the TEX typesetting system, in-house macros, POSTSCRIPT line-drawing macros, and set in the Computer Modern fonts.